W9-CFT-413

Super Problems

Lyle Fisher

DALE
SEYMOUR
PUBLICATIONS
P.O. BOX 10888
PALO ALTO, CA 94303

This book is dedicated to Connee.

Production Coordinator: Ruth Cottrell
Illustrator: Bob Larsen
Cover Art: Julie Peterson

Copyright © 1982 by Dale Seymour Publications. All rights reserved. Printed in the
United States of America. Published simultaneously in Canada.

Limited Reproduction Permission: The authors and publisher hereby grant permission to the teacher who purchases this book, or the teacher for whom the book is
purchased, to reproduce up to 100 copies of any part of this book for use with his or
her students. Any further duplication is prohibited.

ISBN 0-86651-086-9

Order Number DSO1244

efghi-MA-89321098

**DALE
SEYMOUR
PUBLICATIONS**
P.O. BOX 10888
PALO ALTO, CA 94303

CONTENTS

PREFACE

Problem solving is at the core of mathematics. All strands of mathematics should presuppose that problem solving will be an outcome of each. The art of problem solving demands many skills. We should not try to categorize types of problems nor types of solutions. The ability to solve problems comes from experience. We must provide the opportunity for these experiences and allow students to develop their own methods of attacking problems.

Good problems are the essence of teaching problem solving. Each problem should present a new challenge to students and each student should face a new challenge with each problem.

We are becoming an information society and the very accumulation of that information generates new information. The problem solvers of the future will be those who can examine information and look for patterns that suggest solutions. The ability to generalize from specific data may be a better preparation for a student than the continuous repetition of arithmetic skills. It is important to make mathematics vital and exciting, and problem solving is the approach.

Mathematics is a paper and pencil sport. Attempts at designing approaches to solutions demand experimentation. Where long, tedious calculations are an essential part of the problem-solving process we must encourage the use of calculators and computers.

The solutions, hints, and suggestions to teachers are the result of my working with students in grades 5-9. These students are participating in an after-school enrichment program supported by our district schools. Some of the problem ideas were generated by Brother Alfred Brousseau, St. Mary's College, and Harold Andersen, Santa Rosa Junior College. They have given strong support to the Brother Alfred Brousseau Problem Solving Competition sponsored by the California Mathematics Council.

In all my efforts directed toward students in grades 5-9, it would have been an impossible task without the friendship, support, and expertise of Bill Medigovich of the Redwood High School Mathematics Department.

Bill Kennedy, Ed Allen, and George Stratton have assisted by using the problems with their students at Kent Middle School in Larkspur and offering valuable commentary.

L. F.
San Rafael, CA
January 1982

INTRODUCTION

Super Problems is a collection of 16 sets of problems for grades 7–9. Each set of three related problems includes a Warm-up problem, an illustrated Poster problem, and an Extension problem. Accompanying the problem book are the 16 Poster problems, spiral-bound in a calendar-style format, with motivating illustrations in vibrant color for use as classroom posters.

Reproducible worksheets for students

Each of the 48 different problems appears on a separate page with space allowed for students to write their solutions or other notes. Duplicate the pages, and either hand out the problems one at a time, give them as in-class work, or assign them for homework.

Discussions for the teacher

On the back of each student worksheet page is a discussion of the problem including the answer, a detailed solution, hints to help the students get started, background information on the problem, specific teaching suggestions, and ways to extend the problem.

Problem sequence

There is no required order for using the 16 sets of problems. Simply choose those sets that best suit your students' learning situation. But within each set of problems, it is best to assign the Warm-up problem first, then the Poster problem, and finally the Extension problem. It is *not* necessary to use all 48 problems. Sometimes you may use a week or more in worthwhile discussion of a single problem, taking the time to carry that discussion to its fullest.

Focus on problem solving

These problems have been chosen to help you concentrate on the development of students' problem-solving skills rather than on algebraic or geometric structure. Most of the solutions require only the use of basic arithmetic. They may, of course, be solved using algebra or geometry. Students will be able to use the mathematical skills they already have.

Problem-solving strategies

The problems themselves can be solved in more than one way and different problems require different strategies. Some of the strategies that students will find helpful are these:

Look for a pattern.
Guess and check.
Write an equation.
Use logical reasoning.
Work backwards.
Draw a picture.
Make an organized list.
Make a table.
Make a tree diagram.
Use objects or act out the problem.
Solve a simpler related problem.

Suggestions for teaching problem solving.

Problem solving should be a part of every student's daily work. One way is to provide from ten to fifteen minutes of *each* class period for discussion and work on problems. Very few problems are completed in a single period, but this gives students time to digest the problems, think about them, leave them alone, and come back with new, fresh ideas. Make each class like the *Perils of Pauline*, right down to the last minute. That's when you give a good question to ponder, one that students can't quite get out of their minds.

Here are some suggestions that are essential for anyone who is planning to teach problem solving.

Work the problems.
Before assigning a problem to your class, work it yourself. You will have a much better feeling for the problem and be able to anticipate difficulties that students may encounter.

Define the problems.
Carefully discuss the intent of a new problem when you introduce it. Read the problem along with the class and invite questions. Taking care that students understand a problem is essential to their success.

Require records of work.
Encourage students to keep a record of their work on a problem. (The author requires all work on problems to be kept in a spiral notebook.) Students should record all attempts, failures as well as successes. They should give explanations of their thinking. Such records are helpful for later reference and as a needed ingredient for research.

Allow students to devise their own plans.

Different approaches are possible, depending on the insights and skills of each student. Discussions of different ways of looking at a problem are very illuminating to both class and teacher alike.

Look for simpler related problems.

Urge students to look for simpler problems that give insights into the problem at hand. For example ask, "What's the simplest problem? Don't bother with the hard stuff at first." Often a simpler problem provides the key to a solution.

Generalize.

Ask for generalizations, but don't expect rigid, formal statements. In many cases, students will have a feeling for the solution to a problem, but will be unable to completely formalize it. Help them out.

Take time.

Carry discussions to their fullest. Give students the chance to work with a problem and play around with it until something "pops."

Answer questions with questions.

Don't give free information. Students must learn to think and reason through solutions themselves.

Look back at what has been done.

How was the problem solved? Is there another way? Does this look like the solution to any other problem? Does it suggest other problems for investigation?

Be actively involved with a problem.

You can't teach problem solving unless you are involved with it yourself. Work the problems on your own. What are possible approaches? What difficulties will students have? How does it tie into other work students have had? What new problems does it suggest?

Solving a problem may not be fun so much as it is hard work. But the pleasure in reaching a successful solution makes the effort worthwhile.

How many domino pieces (bones) are in a double-six set? Remember that there will be a double-zero, double-one, and so on to double-six, and that one-zero is the same piece as zero-one.

Copyright © 1982 by Dale Seymour Publications.

1. WARM-UP

Answer: 28 pieces

Hint:

Picture the domino pieces.

Solution:

Starting with the double-zero we have:

0,0			
0,1	1,1		
0,2	1,2	2,2	
0,3	1,3	2,3	
0,4	1,4	2,4	
0,5	1,5	2,5	
0,6	1,6	2,6	
7 pieces	6 pieces	5 pieces	

3,3			
3,4	4,4		
3,5	4,5	5,5	
3,6	4,6	5,6	6,6
4 pieces	3 pieces	2 pieces	1 piece

Thus, there are $7 + 6 + 5 + 4 + 3 + 2 + 1 = 28$ pieces.

Teaching Suggestions:

Many of your students will picture the complete set of dominoes just as in the solution shown above. Do not discourage this approach. Grinding out a solution step by step is a very acceptable method. The purpose of this Warm-up problem is to provide a sound basis for understanding *Domino Digs*. This is the simpler case that the students should solve before they attempt the more difficult problem.

Some students may make one major "jump" toward a generalization in this problem. After picturing the first set of dominoes starting with 0,0, and perhaps the second set, those students with insight will move directly to the conclusion that the total number of pieces can be described as $7 + 6 + 5 + 4 + 3 + 2 + 1$.

Occasionally a student will make use of Gauss' summing technique at this point, but this happens more frequently during the solution of *Domino Digs* or its *Extension*.

How many domino pieces (bones) are in a double-fifteen set? Remember that there will be a double-zero, double-one, and so on to double-fifteen, and that one-zero is the same piece as zero-one.

Copyright © 1982 by Dale Seymour Publications.

1. DOMINO DIGS

Answer: 136 pieces

Hints:

Start an organized list of the domino pieces.

Try to avoid listing every single piece by looking for patterns and generalizing.

Solution:

An organized list gives this pattern:

```
0,0
0,1        1,1
0,2        1,2        2,2
0,3        1,3        2,3
0,4        1,4        2,4
 •          •          •
 •          •          •
 •          •          •
0,15       1,15       2,15              15,15
16 pieces  15 pieces  14 pieces   ...   1 piece
```

Thus, we can generalize and say that the set contains $16 + 15 + 14 + \ldots + 2 + 1 = 136$ pieces.

Teaching Suggestions:

Making an organized list is an important problem-solving technique for students to learn. Spend some time discussing the different ways they organized the data for themselves. Focus their attention on the patterns that appear in their lists.

The computation of the sum $16 + 15 + \ldots + 1$ presents an opportunity for the students to discover and generalize a useful concept in the study of number theory. At the age of 10, Karl Gauss (1777–1855) expressed a formula for the sum $1 + 2 + 3 + \ldots + n$. Begin with simple sums and help your students follow Gauss' line of reasoning.

	Sum
$n = 1$	1
$n = 2$	$1 + 2 = 3$
$n = 3$	$1 + 2 + 3 = 6$
$n = 4$	$1 + 2 + 3 + 4 = 10$
$n = 5$	$1 + 2 + 3 + 4 + 5 = 15$
$n = 6$	$1 + 2 + 3 + 4 + 5 + 6 = 21$

For $n = 5$ and $n = 6$, Gauss observed the following:

$$\begin{array}{c} 1 + 2 + 3 + 4 + 5 \\ 5 + 4 + 3 + 2 + 1 \\ \hline 6 + 6 + 6 + 6 + 6 = 5 \times 6 = 30 \end{array}$$

The sum $1 + 2 + 3 + 4 + 5 = 15$ or $\frac{1}{2} \times 30$.

$$\begin{array}{c} 1 + 2 + 3 + 4 + 5 + 6 \\ 6 + 5 + 4 + 3 + 2 + 1 \\ \hline 7 + 7 + 7 + 7 + 7 + 7 = 6 \times 7 = 42 \end{array}$$

The sum $1 + 2 + \ldots + 6 = 21$ or $\frac{1}{2} \times 42$.

Use several examples before generalizing.

The sum of the first and last terms multiplied by the number of terms will be exactly twice the sum of the terms.

So we have the formula $1 + 2 + \ldots + n = \dfrac{n(n + 1)}{2}$

Here are three extension problems you might give for more practice on Gauss' technique.

a) $24 + 26 + 28 + 30 + \ldots + 46$
b) $1 + 3 + 5 + 7 + \ldots + 35$
c) $1 + 4 + 7 + 10 + \ldots + 28$

Answers: a) $\dfrac{12 \times (24 + 46)}{2} = 420$

b) $\dfrac{18 \times (1 + 35)}{2} = 324$

c) $\dfrac{10 \times (1 + 28)}{2} = 145$

The numbers in the sequence 1, 1, 2, 3, 5, 8, 13, ... are called Fibonacci numbers. The starting numbers are 1, 1. Every other number in the sequence is the sum of the two preceding numbers. That is, $2 = 1 + 1, 3 = 1 + 2, 5 = 2 + 3, 8 = 3 + 5$, and $13 = 5 + 8$. What is the sum of the squares of the first 20 Fibonacci numbers? (Use the table below.)

n	Fibonacci number	Square of Fibonacci number	Sum of first n Fibonacci squares	Factors of sum of first n Fibonacci squares
1	1	1	1	1×1
2	1	1	2	1×2
3	2	4	6	2×3
4	3	9	15	
5	5	25		
6	8			
7	13			
8				
9				
10				
11				
12				
13				
14				
15				
16				
17				
18				
19				
20				

Copyright © 1982 by Dale Seymour Publications.

1. EXTENSION

Answer:

n	Fibonacci number	Square of Fibonacci number	Sum of first n Fibonacci squares	Factors of sum of first n Fibonacci squares
1	1	1	1	1×1
2	1	1	2	1×2
3	2	4	6	2×3
4	3	9	15	3×5
5	5	25	40	5×8
6	8	64	104	8×13
7	13	169	273	13×21
8	21	441	714	21×34
9	34	1156	1870	34×55
10	55	3025	4895	55×89
11	89	7921	12816	89×144
12	144	20736	33552	144×233
13	233	54289	87841	233×377
14	377	142129	229970	377×610
15	610	372100	602070	610×987
16	987	974169	1576239	987×1597
17	1597	2550409	4126648	1597×2584
18	2584	6677056	10803704	2584×4181
19	4181	17480761	28284465	4181×6765
20	6765	45765225	74049690	6765×10946
21	10946			

Hints:

Complete the table one row at a time.

Look for patterns that might eliminate the need for some of the calculations.

Solution:

All the squares and summations are shown in the table above, because some students may complete the entire table. Hopefully, students will discover the pattern that the sum of the first n Fibonacci squares equals the product of the nth Fibonacci number (F_n) and the $(n+1)$th Fibonacci number (F_{n+1}). This discovery will shorten the tedious calculation of the sum of the first 20 Fibonacci squares considerably.

Teaching Suggestions:

Looking for patterns is one of the most important techniques of problem solving. Many of the problems in this book have been selected specifically to encourage students to look for patterns.

Working row-by-row rather than column-by-column, my students discovered the pattern of factors before they reached the tenth row in the table. They then skipped the other rows, found the twenty-first Fibonacci number, and the resulting product $F_{20} \times F_{21}$. Students who solve the problem this way should be able to generalize that the sum of the first n Fibonacci squares is $F_n \times F_{n+1}$.

An interesting extension to this problem is to have the students write a computer program to generate the set of Fibonacci numbers, and perhaps some of the other columns in the table as well.

Two dice are shown below with their sides unfolded so that you can see the numbers on all sides. Suppose you roll the two dice. How many different pairs of numbers can you possibly roll?

When two dice are rolled, the one showing the greater number is considered the winner. In how many cases would the red die win over the green die? In how many cases would the green die win over the red die? Would there be any ties?

Red die

	3	
1	9	11
	2	
	10	

Green die

	14	
5	3	11
	12	
	4	

Copyright © 1982 by Dale Seymour Publications.

Answers: There are 36 different pairs.

Red die wins 9 times.

Green die wins 25 times.

There are 2 ties.

Hint:

Make an organized listing of all the ways in which the numbers on the two dice can come up.

Solution:

With each of the six numbers on the red die, any of the six numbers on the green die can be paired. A partial listing of the 36 possible pairings and the winner of the toss is shown below.

Red	Green	Winner
3	4	green
3	5	green
3	3	tie
3	11	green
3	12	green
3	14	green
9	4	red
9	5	red
9	3	red
9	11	green
9	12	green
9	14	green
•	•	•
•	•	•
•	•	•

By counting the entries in the Winner column, we find that the red die wins 9 times, the green die wins 25 times, and there are 2 ties.

Teaching Suggestions:

Although the answers can certainly be found from the complete organized listing of the pairings, it is advantageous to rearrange the information in such a way that the number of red wins, green wins, and ties are more easily counted.

Roll of red die	Number of times		
	red wins	green wins	tie
3	0	5	1
9	3	3	0
1	0	6	0
11	3	2	1
2	0	6	0
10	3	3	0
Totals:	9	25	2

This type of table will be helpful to students in organizing their solutions to *Samantha's Experiment* and its *Extension*.

Following the discussion of this problem, you may wish to introduce the idea of probability. Here we have

$$P \text{ (red wins)} = \frac{\text{Number of ways red can win}}{\text{Total number of pairings}} = \frac{9}{36}$$

$$P \text{ (green wins)} = \frac{\text{Number of ways green can win}}{\text{Total number of pairings}} = \frac{25}{36}$$

$$P \text{ (tie)} = \frac{\text{Number of ways a tie can occur}}{\text{Total number of pairings}} = \frac{2}{36}$$

Samantha is experimenting with three spinners. Each spinner is divided into three equal sections with a number in each section. Spinner A shows 8, 6, 1; spinner B shows 7, 5, 3; spinner C shows 9, 4, 2. Samantha spins two spinners and records as winner the one that stopped on the greater number. She has already found that A usually wins over B and that B usually wins over C. She guesses that A will usually win over C. Is her guess correct?

Find the probabilities that A wins over B and that B wins over C. If spinners A and C are spun, which one do you think will win most often?

Copyright © 1982 by Dale Seymour Publications.

2. SAMANTHA'S EXPERIMENT

Answers: No.

$P(A$ wins over $B) = 5/9$

$P(B$ wins over $C) = 5/9$

C will usually win over A because $P(C$ wins over $A) = 5/9$.

Hints:

How many different pairs of numbers can be spun on spinners A and B? B and C? C and A?

In each case, which spinner wins?

Solution:

Examine spinner A versus spinner B.

Spin of A	Number of times	
	A wins	B wins
8	3	0
6	2	1
1	0	3
Totals:	5	4

There are $5 + 4 = 9$ different pairs of numbers which can be spun. Thus the probability of A winning over B is 5/9.

Examine spinner B versus spinner C.

Spin of B	Number of times	
	B wins	C wins
7	2	1
5	2	1
3	1	2
Totals:	5	4

The probability of B winning over C is 5/9.

Examine spinner C versus spinner A.

Spin of C	Number of times	
	C wins	A wins
9	3	0
4	1	2
2	1	2
Totals:	5	4

The probability of C winning over A is 5/9.

Thus Samantha's guess that A would usually win over C was incorrect.

Teaching Suggestions:

Before giving this problem, you may wish to have the students make a set of the spinners A, B, and C and perform the probability experiment. This is a good opportunity for students to see how the theoretical probability and the experimental results compare.

Some students may need to list the pairings for spinners A and B, B and C, C and A before creating tables such as the ones used in the solution.

Be sure that the students are familiar with the basic definition of the probability of an event.

This is a good opportunity to review the transitive properties of equality and order for real numbers:

If $a = b$ and $b = c$, then $a = c$.

If $a > b$ and $b > c$, then $a > c$.

If $a < b$ and $b < c$, then $a < c$.

Samantha's guess that spinner A would usually win over C is based on her assumption that the situation is transitive, but the solution shows that this particular probability situation is nontransitive. The *Extension* problem offers another nontransitive probability situation for students to explore.

Each set of four dice shown unfolded below illustrates a non-transitive situation. That is, if the dice are rolled in pairs, the chances are that A will defeat B, B will defeat C, C will defeat D, and surprisingly, D will defeat A. For each set of dice, what is the probability that A will defeat B? B will defeat C? C will defeat D? D will defeat A?

Set 1

```
        0                 3                 2                 5
   4    0    4       3    3    3       2    6    2       5    1    1
        4                 3                 2                 5
        4                 3                 6                 1
        A                 B                 C                 D
```

Set 2

```
        2                 0                 6                 4
   3    9    3       1    8    7       6    5    6       4   12    4
       10                 8                 6                 4
       11                 8                 5                12
        A                 B                 C                 D
```

Copyright © 1982 by Dale Seymour Publications.

2. EXTENSION

Answers: A. The probability is 2/3 in each case.

B. The probability is 2/3 in each case.

Solution:

A. Examine *A* versus *B*.

Roll of *A*	Number of times	
	A wins	*B* wins
4	6	0
4	6	0
4	6	0
4	6	0
0	0	6
0	0	6
Totals:	24	12

The probability that *A* will defeat *B* is 24/36 or 2/3.

Similar tables can be created for *B* versus *C*, *C* versus *D*, and *D* versus *A*. The probabilities that *B* will defeat *C*, that *C* will defeat *D*, and that *D* will defeat *A* are all equal to 24/36 or 2/3.

B. Examine *A* versus *B*.

Roll of *A*	Number of times	
	A wins	*B* wins
2	2	4
3	2	4
3	2	4
9	6	0
10	6	0
11	6	0
Totals:	24	12

The probability that *A* will defeat *B* is 24/36 or 2/3.

Similar tables can be created for *B* versus *C*, *C* versus *D*, and *D* versus *A*. The probabilities that *B* will defeat *C*, that *C* will defeat *D*, and that *D* will defeat *A* are all equal to 24/36 or 2/3.

Teaching Suggestions:

Before introducing this problem, you may wish to obtain some unmarked dice and set up the two probability experiments. Have the students perform the experiments and then compare their experimental results with the theoretical probabilities.

Here is an extension problem that may intrigue your students.

Given three spinners *A*, *B*, and *C* with each spinner divided into five equal parts. Using each of the whole numbers from 1 through 15 once, can you arrange the numbers on the wheels so that the chances are in favor of spinner *A* winning over *B*, *B* winning over *C*, and *C* winning over *A*? State the probabilities associated with your arrangement of the numbers.

There are many possible arrangements. One is

Spinner *A*: 15, 10, 9, 4, 2

Spinner *B*: 14, 11, 8, 6, 1

Spinner *C*: 13, 12, 7, 5, 3

A strip of paper has *n* spaces. In each space we write 1 or 0, with the restriction that no two 1s may be written next to each other. The number *T(n)* represents all the different ways in which the 1s and 0s can be placed on a strip with *n* spaces. Find the values of *T(n)* for *n* = 1, 2, 3, ..., 7. Describe a general rule for finding *T(n)*.

n	T(n)
1	2
2	
3	
4	
5	
6	
7	

| 0 |

| 1 |

| 0 | 1 |

| | |

| | |

Copyright © 1982 by Dale Seymour Publications.

3. WARM-UP

Answer:

n	T(n)
1	2
2	3
3	5
4	8
5	13
6	21
7	34

The rule is $T(n) = T(n - 1) + T(n - 2)$ for $n \geq 3$.

Hint:

Draw the arrangements and look for patterns.

Solution:

For $n = 1$, we have 2 possible arrangements.
  (0), (1)

For $n = 2$, we have 3 possible arrangements.
  (0,0), (0,1), (1,0)

For $n = 3$, we have 5 possible arrangements.
  (0,0,0)
  (0,0,1)
  (0,1,0)
  (1,0,0)
  (1,0,1)

For $n = 4$, we have 8 possible arrangements.
  (0,0,0,0)
  (0,0,0,1)
  (0,0,1,0)
  (0,1,0,0)
  (0,1,0,1)
  (1,0,0,0)
  (1,0,0,1)
  (1,0,1,0)

For $n = 5$, we have 13 possible arrangements.
  Eight are repetitions of $n = 4$, each preceded by 0.
  (0,0,0,0,0)
  (0,0,0,0,1)
  (0,0,0,1,0)
  (0,0,1,0,0)
  (0,0,1,0,1)
  (0,1,0,0,0)
  (0,1,0,0,1)
  (0,1,0,1,0)

Five are repetitions of $n = 3$, each preceded by 1,0.
(1,0,0,0,0)
(1,0,0,0,1)
(1,0,0,1,0)
(1,0,1,0,0)
(1,0,1,0,1)

For $n = 6$, the 13 arrangements for $n = 5$ are repeated, each preceded by 0, and the 8 arrangements for $n = 4$ are repeated, each preceded by 1,0. Thus, there are 21 possible arrangements.

For $n = 7$, the 21 arrangements for $n = 6$ are repeated, each preceded by 0, and the 13 arrangements for $n = 5$ are repeated, each preceded by 1,0. Thus, there are 34 possible arrangements.

Teaching Suggestions:

If students keep a notebook of their solutions, this problem will serve as a ready reminder for other problems. In particular, this problem serves as an introduction to *Future Attractions*.

Students who have previously encountered the set of Fibonacci numbers (see *1. Extension*) may jump to a rule after finding the first three or four values of $T(n)$. Others will see that $T(n)$ is the sum of the two previous values, in a step or two more.

Binary numbers are numbers that use only the digits 0 and 1. There are four two-digit binary numbers: 00, 01, 10, and 11. In the figure below the four numbers have been placed around a circle in such a way that any two adjacent numbers differ in only one digit.

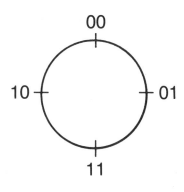

There are eight three-digit binary numbers: 000, 001, 010, 011, 100, 101, 110, and 111. Can you place these eight numbers around a circle in such a way that any two adjacent numbers differ in only one digit? Is a similar arrangement possible for the sixteen four-digit binary numbers?

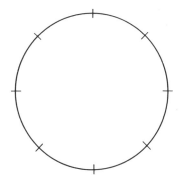
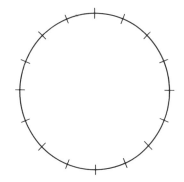

Copyright © 1982 by Dale Seymour Publications.

3. FUTURE ATTRACTIONS

Answers: One possible answer is shown below for each problem.

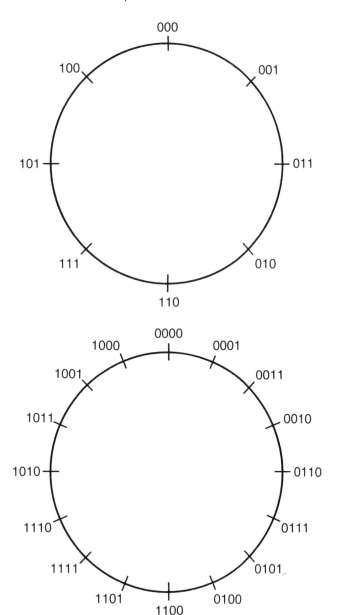

Hint:

Write the binary numbers on slips of paper to experiment with different arrangements.

Solution:

The three-digit arrangement is closely related to the two-digit arrangement. Counting clockwise, the four-point circle arrangement of the two-digit numbers is
  00-01-11-10.
The eight-point circle counting to the right reads in this same pattern, but with a 0 in the left-hand digit.
  000-001-011-010.
Counting to the left on the eight-point circle, place a 1 in the left-hand digit and then repeat the two-digit sequence.
  100-101-111-110

This pattern extends to the arrangement of the four-digit binary numbers on the 16-point circle. Counting to the right on the 16-point circle, place 0 in the left-hand digit and then use the three-digit sequence.
  0000-0001-0011-0010-0110-0111-0101-0100
Counting to the left, change the left-hand digit to 1, and then repeat the three-digit sequence.
  1000-1001-1011-1010-1110-1111-1101-1100

Teaching Suggestions:

This problem can be a starting point for the discussion of place value, addition, subtraction, multiplication and division of binary numbers.

There is more than one correct answer for each of the arrangements. Encourage the students to compare their solutions.

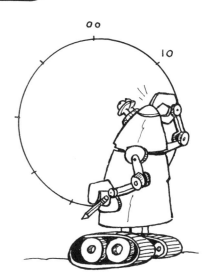

Numbers written in base three use only the digits 0, 1, and 2. There are nine two-digit base three numbers: 00, 01, 02, 10, 11, 12, 20, 21, and 22. Determine whether these numbers can be placed around a circle in such a way that any two adjacent numbers differ in only one digit.

Is a similar arrangement possible for the 27 three-digit base three numbers?

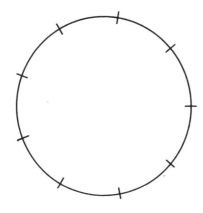

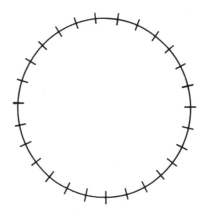

Copyright © 1982 by Dale Seymour Publications.

Discussion for

3. EXTENSION

Answers: Several correct arrangements are possible. One arrangement is shown below for each of the two problems.

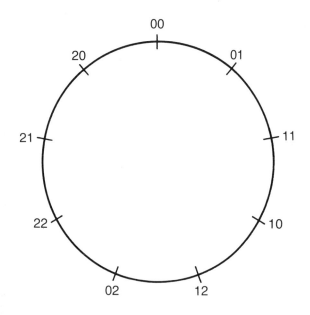

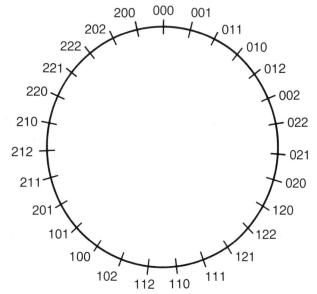

Solution:

The only caution in planning a solution for the three-digit problem is to have two zeroes in the final arrangement in order to get back to 000 according to the rules.

Teaching Suggestions:

Encourage the students to approach this problem in the same way as they did *Future Attractions.*

This problem provides an opportunity to further solidify the concept of number bases and place values. You may wish to create a few problems involving basic arithmetic operations in base three.

Consider numbers of the form 2^n, where $n = 1$, 2, 3, 4, 5, ... Find a pattern in the units digits of 2^n. What will be the units digit of 2^{31921}?

Copyright © 1982 by Dale Seymour Publications.

4. WARM-UP

Answers: All powers of two have a units digit ending in 2, 4, 8, 6.

The units digit of 2^{31921} is 2.

Hint:

Use a calculator to make a table of the powers of 2.

Solution:

An examination of the units digits of the powers of 2 reveals the pattern.

n	2^n
1	2
2	4
3	8
4	16
5	32
6	64
7	128
8	256
9	512
10	1024
11	2048
12	4096
13	8192
•	•
•	•
•	•

Students will make the conjecture that the repeating pattern for the units digit is 2, 4, 8, 6, 2, 4, 8, 6, ...

The value for 2^{31921} cannot be computed on a hand-held calculator. Therefore, an examination of n in 2^n is necessary.

n	Remainder of $n \div 4$	Units digit of 2^n
1	1	2
2	2	4
3	3	8
4	0	6
5	1	2
6	2	4
7	3	8
8	0	6
9	1	1
•	•	•
•	•	•
•	•	•

The conclusion to be drawn from examination of this table is that if the exponent is divided by 4, the remainder and units digit show the following pattern.

Remainder	Units digit
1	2
2	4
3	8
0	6

Since $31921 \div 4 = 7980$, remainder 1, the units digit of 2^{31921} is 2.

Teaching Suggestions:

Students will not have difficulty in determining the pattern of the units digits. It is a good idea to have them show the repetition of the pattern for at least three or four sequences. This is a good time to point out the value of the calculator.

Difficulty may arise for some students in the examination of the exponents. You may need to ask one or two leading questions to turn their efforts in the right direction. But don't tell them! They will discover the table on their own, given time.

As an extension, ask the students to observe other possible patterns in the table of powers of two. Let them be creative. For example, some students in my class found that the sum of the digits of the powers of two created the repeating pattern 1, 2, 4, 8, 7, 5.

The wizard has been imprisoned by a powerful spell. To escape he must find the quickest way to move the tower of ten disks from one post to another such that the disks have the same arrangement as on the original post. He may move only one disk at a time, and he may never place a larger disk on top of a smaller one. What is the minimum number of moves he must make in order to move the ten-disk tower?

Copyright © 1982 by Dale Seymour Publications.

4. WIZARD'S TOWER

Answer: 1023 moves

Hints:

Make a model of the problem.

Look at the simpler related problems of moving a one-disk tower, a two-disk tower, a three-disk tower, and so on.

Make a table of the number of disks and the matching minimum number of disk moves. Look for patterns.

Solution:

Use a model to find the minimum number of disk moves for towers of one, two, three, and four disks. Now is the time to teach a major point in problem solving: The problem solver should always look back. Does the set of answers relate to any previous work we have done? Problem *4. Warm-up* gave us a table relating to 2^n. How does this table relate to the minimum number of disk moves? Once the relationship is determined, the pattern $2^n - 1$ is a simple jump for students.

Number of disks	Minimum number of disk moves	Pattern
1	1	$2^1 - 1$
2	3	$2^2 - 1$
3	7	$2^3 - 1$
4	15	$2^4 - 1$
5	31	$2^5 - 1$
6	63	$2^6 - 1$
7	127	$2^7 - 1$
8	255	$2^8 - 1$
9	511	$2^9 - 1$
10	1023	$2^{10} - 1$

Teaching Suggestions:

Explain the rules carefully. Students need to understand what is meant by keeping the disks in the same arrangement, from smallest to largest on the post.

It is important to use a model for this problem. Here are some possibilities.

  a. This puzzle, sometimes called the "Tower of Hanoi," can be purchased at most toy and game stores.

  b. Cut out circles from paper or tagboard to construct a model.

  c. The problem can be modeled using only paper and pencil, as shown below for the four-disk tower.

Start:

```
1
2
3
4
____    ____    ____
Post A  Post B  Post C
```

Move disk 1 to post *C*, 2 to *B*, then 1 to *B*. Notice that the number of slashes equals the number of moves made.

```
1̸
2̸
3       1
4       2       1̸
____    ____    ____
Post A  Post B  Post C
```

Now move disk 3 to post *C*, 1 to *A*, 2 to *C*, then 1 back to *C*.

```
1̸
1̸              1
2̸              2
3̸      1̸       3
4       2       1̸
____    ____    ____
Post A  Post B  Post C
```

Now move 4 to *B*, 1 to *B*, then 2 to *A*.

```
2
1̸
1̸      1       1̸
2̸      4       2̸
3̸      1̸      3
4̸      2       1̸
____    ____    ____
Post A  Post B  Post C
```

Now move 1 to *A*, 3 to *B*, then 1 to *C*.

```
1̸
2
1̸      3       1
1̸      1̸      1̸
2̸      4       2̸
3̸      1̸      3̸
4̸      2       1̸
____    ____    ____
Post A  Post B  Post C
```

Now move 2 to *B* and finally 1 to *B*.

```
1̸      1
2̸      2
1̸      3
1̸      1̸      1̸
2̸      4       2̸
3̸      1̸      3̸
4̸      2       1̸
____    ____    ____
Post A  Post B  Post C
```

Count the number of slashes and you have the correct number of moves, 15. I like this method because it uses only one chart and the number of moves is easily counted.

Let us continue the tower problem begun in problem *4. Wizard's Tower.* In a 32-disk tower, what would be the minimum number of disk moves required? If each move takes one second, about how many years will it take to move a 32-disk tower? In an *n*-disk tower, what would be the minimum number of moves required?

Copyright © 1982 by Dale Seymour Publications.

4. EXTENSION

Answers: $2^{32} - 1$ moves

136 years

$2^{n} - 1$ moves

Teaching Suggestions:

The calculator is a valuable tool both for factoring and long division in this problem.

Solution:

The minimum number of moves for a 32-disk tower, following the pattern $2^{n} - 1$ developed in *Wizard's Tower,* is $2^{32} - 1$, or approximately 2^{32}. The number of years required to make 2^{32} moves at a rate of one move per second is calculated below.

$$\frac{\text{minimum number of moves}}{\text{number of seconds per year}}$$

$$= \frac{2^{32}}{60 \text{ seconds} \times 60 \text{ minutes} \times 24 \text{ hours} \times 365 \text{ days}}$$

$$= \frac{2^{32}}{60 \times 60 \times 24 \times 365}$$

$$= \frac{2^{32}}{2^{7} \times 3^{3} \times 5^{3} \times 73}$$

$$= \frac{2^{25}}{3^{3} \times 5^{3} \times 73} = \frac{33,554,432}{246,375}$$

$$= 136.19251 \text{ or approximately 136 years}$$

At the last school board election in Angletown, 4620 votes were cast. Candidate Acute received 236 votes more than candidate Obtuse. Candidate Right received 698 votes more than candidate Acute. Candidate Straight received 256 votes less than candidate Right. How many votes did each receive?

Copyright © 1982 by Dale Seymour Publications.

Discussion for

5. WARM-UP

Answer: Obtuse — 693 votes
Acute — 929 votes
Right — 1627 votes
Straight — 1371 votes

Solution:

For those students who have not yet studied formal algebra, a thorough discussion of the steps in the solution will help them to understand the reasoning.

First, make a list of how many votes each candidate received. Since we don't know how many votes Obtuse received, we'll call that N for the time being. Now, how many votes did Acute receive? Right? Straight?

Obtuse: N votes
Acute: Obtuse $+ 236 = N + 236$
Right: Acute $+ 698 = (N + 236) + 698 = N + 934$
Straight: Right $- 256 = (N + 934) - 256 = N + 678$

Next, find the total number of votes.

$$\begin{array}{l} N \\ N + 236 \\ N + 934 \\ \underline{N + 678} \\ 4 \times N + 1848 = 4620 \text{ votes} \end{array}$$

So $4 \times N = 4620 - 1848 = 2772$, and $N = 2772 \div 4 =$ 693 votes for Obtuse.

Now that we know the value for N, we can find the remaining answers.

Acute received $693 + 236 = 929$ votes.
Right received $929 + 698 = 1627$ votes.
Straight received $1627 - 256 = 1371$ votes.

Teaching Suggestions:

Here is an opportunity to review the associative property of addition in the context of problem solving. A few arithmetic examples should suffice.

This can be followed by either an introduction or a review of the addition and multiplication properties of equality. If you are introducing the addition property, take the time to use a physical model such as a balance scale.

The political commentator on station KNYN summarized an election result as follows:

"A Tail Wagger Party victory of 1,729 votes in the last election has been turned into a Rescuer Party victory of 1,654 in this election. The Rescuer Party candidate received 38% of the votes cast. The Tail Wagger Party candidate finished in second place. The Best Friend Party received only 14% of the votes cast and was beaten for third place by the Sheepherder Party by 50 votes."

If there were only four candidates in the election, determine the number of votes each candidate received.

Copyright © 1982 by Dale Seymour Publications.

Answer: Rescuer Party — 15,238 votes

Tail Wagger Party — 13,584 votes

Best Friend Party — 5,614 votes

Sheepherder Party — 5,664 votes

Solution:

Let N = total number of votes cast

$\frac{38}{100}N$ = Rescuer Party votes

$\frac{38}{100}N - 1654$ = Tail Wagger Party votes

$\frac{14}{100}N$ = Best Friend Party votes

$\frac{14}{100}N + 50$ = Sheepherder votes

$\frac{38}{100}N + \frac{38}{100}N - 1654 + \frac{14}{100}N + \frac{14}{100}N + 50 = N$

$\frac{104}{100}N - 1604 = N$

$\frac{4}{100}N = 1604$

$N = 40,100$

Then we have,

  $38\% \times 40,100 = 15,238$ (Rescuer)

  $15,238 - 1,654 = 13,584$ (Tail Wagger)

  $14\% \times 40,100 = 5,614$ (Best Friend)

  $5,614 + 50 = 5,664$ (Sheepherder)

Teaching Suggestions:

This problem provides an opportunity to relate problem solving to the maintenance of decimal or fraction skills. The original equation could be written $.38N + .38N - 1654 + .14N + .14N + 50 = N$.

This is an excellent problem for using estimation and calculators. This approach eliminates the need for students to be able to solve equations algebraically. After setting up the original equation, my students simplified it to $1.04N - 1604 = N$, and then tried the following "guesstimation" process.

"Will the total number of votes cast be less than or greater than 10,000?" We agreed that 10,000 might be a good guess, and tried it.

  $1.04(10,000) - 1064 = 10,000$

  $8,796 = 10,000$ (Not a correct guess.)

"Should the next guess be greater or less than 10,000?" There was some agreement that the guess should be greater, but with no high degree of certainty. So we tried 20,000.

  $1.04(20,000) - 1604 = 20,000$

  $19,196 = 20,000$

We were "closer" to equality so now the class felt certain that the number was greater than 20,000. Our next guess was 30,000.

  $1.04(30,000) - 1604 = 30,000$

  $29,596 = 30,000$

We were much "closer." We then discussed what would happen if our guess were too large. We concluded that in that case the left-hand side of the equation would become greater than the right-hand side. That would indicate that the number N was between the last two guesses. Our next guess was 40,000.

  $1.04(40,000) - 1604 = 40,000$

  $39,996 = 40,000$

Now the class knew they were very close. A few students immediately related the 4-vote difference to .04 as four of a hundred and persuaded the class that 40,100 should be our next guess.

  $1.04(40,100) - 1604 = 40,100$

  $41,704 - 1604 = 40,100$

  $40,100 = 40,100$ (Eureka!)

The solution was now a matter of arithmetic skills.

At a Forest Service Youth Camp many of the workers ate some meals away from the base camp. In the dining hall at the base camp, 5% of the workers had breakfast only, 3% had lunch only, and 2% had supper only. Just 10% of the workers ate all three meals in camp. There were 5,000 meals served at the base camp dining hall. No worker missed all three meals. How many workers were assigned to the Youth Camp?

Copyright © 1982 by Dale Seymour Publications.

5. EXTENSION

Answer: 2500 workers

Hint:

What is the relationship between the number of workers and the number of meals served?

Solution:

Let x = total number of workers in camp
$.05x$ = number eating breakfast only (1 meal)
$.03x$ = number eating lunch only (1 meal)
$.02x$ = number eating supper only (1 meal)
$.10x$ = number eating all 3 meals
Then, $x - .05x - .03x - .02x - .10x = .80x$ = number eating exactly 2 meals.

The number of meals eaten in camp was
$.05x(1) + .03x(1) + .02x(1) + .10x(3) + .80x(2) = 5000$
$2x = 5000$
$x = 2500$ workers assigned to the camp

Teaching Suggestions:

The key to establishing a correct equation is relating the number of workers to the number of meals. Thus, the number of workers eating three meals (10%) must be multiplied by 3 and the number eating two meals (80%) must be multiplied by 2.

Many students will solve this using a trial and error method. They will estimate that the number of workers must be less than the number of meals. A first guess might be 3000 workers. This gives a result of 6000 meals, so a lower guess is necessary. If the next guess is 2000 workers, the resulting number of meals is 4000. Since 5000 is halfway between 4000 and 6000, a good guess would be 2500 workers, which produces the correct number of meals.

A group of students whose knowledge of percents was limited, devised yet another solution. Since the problem was written using percents, the students assumed that there were 100 workers in the camp. Then 10 workers had one meal, 10 had three meals, and 80 had two meals. So there were $10 + 3 \times 10 + 2 \times 80 = 200$ meals eaten by the 100 workers. This meant that the number of workers was just half the number of meals. Thus, if there were 5000 meals served, there must have been 2500 workers.

The figure below is a regular six-pointed star. If the area of the shaded triangle is one square unit, what is the area of the entire star? Point 0 is equidistant from the outer vertices of the star. What is the relationship between the lengths AB and AO?

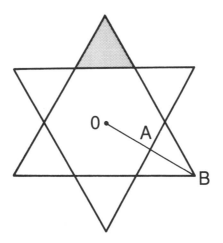

Cop

6. WARM-UP

Answers: The area of the star is 12 square units.

The lengths *AB* and *AO* are equal.

Solution:

By connecting the vertices of the hexagon, we can see that there are 12 equilateral triangles, all the same size, that make up the area of the star. Thus, the area of the star is 12 times the area of one triangle, or 12 square units.

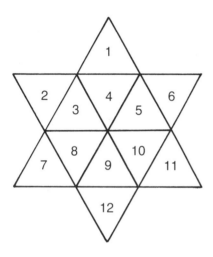

Segments *AB* and *AO* are each altitudes of the equilateral triangles, and hence are the same length.

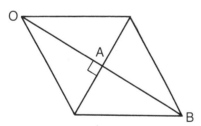

Teaching Suggestions:

A good starting point for this problem is to have the students devise methods of carefully drawing the figure for this problem. It may be the only catalyst needed to start the discussions. Once the diagonals of the hexagon are drawn, many intuitive ideas may surface. Just a few of the exciting thoughts that came out in one of my classes were:

Opposite angles of a parallelogram are congruent.

Vertical angles are congruent.

The concept of a straight angle and its measure.

The six-pointed regular star is formed by two interlocking equilateral triangles.

Don't worry about proof. Most of my students' discoveries were prefaced by such phrases as "It seems that," or "It just has to be true that," or "I drew the figure and it worked." Let the students blast away with their ideas. I was amazed by the reasoning that verged on formal proof. On more than one occasion my only comment to a student was, "You have just discovered what Euclid, Pythagoras, and a few other mathematicians in between have visualized." The students' pride in discovery is just as important to them as it was to the great mathematicians.

If you want to continue a discussion that has been exciting, dust off an old globe and create the triangle formed by two longitudes and the equator. Could you have an equilateral triangle with three right angles? This will probably be the first opportunity for students to encounter a "non-Euclidean" geometry. After all, we know that all triangles have an angle sum of 180°. Or do we?

The design below is a regular six-pointed star drawn inside a circle of radius approximately 34.6 centimeters. If each side of the star is 20 centimeters long, what is the total area of the shaded portion to the nearest hundredth square centimeter? (Use 3.14 for pi.)

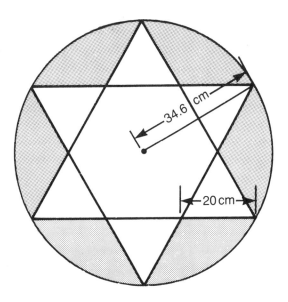

Copyright © 1982 by Dale Seymour Publications.

6. STELLAR VIEW

Answer: 1683.08 square centimeters

Hints:

Find the areas of the star and the circle.

Use the relationships found in problem *6. Warm-up.*

Solution:

To find the area of the star, first find the area of one of the equilateral triangular points. The side, or base of the triangle is 20 cm. The altitude is half the radius of the circle, or 17.3 cm. The area of one triangle is .5 × 20 × 17.3 = 173 square centimeters. We know from problem *6. Warm-up* that the area of the star is 12 × 173 = 2076 square centimeters.

The area of the circle is approximately 3.14 × 34.6 × 34.6 = 3759.08 square centimeters.

Thus, the area of the shaded portion is the difference between the areas of the circle and star, or 3759.08 − 2076 = 1683.08 square centimeters.

Teaching Suggestions:

This is a good time to review the area formulas for triangles and circles.

An extension problem is to find the length of leading required to make all the straight and curved lines in such a stained-glass design.

A regular hexagon can be divided into six equilateral triangles by connecting vertices as shown in the figure below.

A. Given a regular hexagon of side 2, how many equilateral triangles of side 1 can be formed?
B. Given a regular hexagon of side 9, how many equilateral triangles of side 1 can be formed?
C. Given a regular hexagon of side n, how many equilateral triangles of side 1 can be formed?

Copyright © 1982 by Dale Seymour Publications.

6. EXTENSION

Answers: A. 24

B. 486

C. $6n^2$

Hints:

Make a table showing the length of one side of the hexagon and the corresponding number of equilateral triangles of side 1. Then look for patterns.

Think about separating each hexagon into six equilateral triangles by drawing the diagonals of the hexagon. Then count the number of equilateral triangles of side 1 within each of those six larger equilateral triangles.

Solution:

A. The hexagon of side 2 contains six equilateral triangles of side 2. Each of these equilateral triangles can be divided into four equilateral triangles of side 1 as shown below. Hence there are $6 \times 4 = 24$ equilateral triangles of side 1 in the hexagon of side 2.

B. Before proceeding to the hexagon of side 9, it is advantageous to complete the table and see if a pattern evolves. The total number of equilateral triangles of side 1 in the hexagon is equal to six times the number of equilateral triangles of side 1 within each of the six large triangles formed by the diagonals of the hexagon. So we look first at the number of equilateral triangles within just one of those large triangles.

An equilateral triangle of side 1 contains one equilateral triangle of side 1.

As shown in part A, an equilateral triangle of side 2 contains four equilateral triangles of side 1.

Notice that in an equilateral triangle of side 3, there are three rows of the equilateral triangles of side 1. The small triangles can be counted in rows. $1 + 3 + 5 = 9$ equilateral triangles of side 1.

In an equilateral triangle of side 4, the pattern of counting by rows continues. There are $1 + 3 + 5 + 7 = 16$ equilateral triangles of side 1.

Now we can make the table and look for patterns to help us extend it.

Side of hexagon	Number of equil. triangles in each larger equil. triangle	Number of equil. triangles in hexagon (multiply by 6)
1	$1 = 1 = 1^2$	6
2	$1 + 3 = 4 = 2^2$	24
3	$1 + 3 + 5 = 9 = 3^2$	54
4	$1 + 3 + 5 + 7 = 16 = 4^2$	96
5	$1 + 3 + \ldots + 9 = 25 = 5^2$	150
6	$1 + 3 + \ldots + 11 = 36 = 6^2$	216
7	$1 + 3 + \ldots + 13 = 49 = 7^2$	294
8	$1 + 3 + \ldots + 15 = 64 = 8^2$	384
9	$1 + 3 + \ldots + 17 = 81 = 9^2$	486
•	•	•
•	•	•
•	•	•
n	n^2	$6n^2$

C. Using the pattern developed in the table, there are $6n^2$ equilateral triangles of side 1 in any hexagon of side n.

Teaching Suggestions:

Stress that it is most important to start with the simplest case of a side of 1 and build to a pattern of perfect square numbers. This quickly leads to a formula for all cases.

Notice also that in the table we can see that the sum of the first n odd numbers equals the square of the number n.

A. Consider numbers of the form $N = 2 \times 3 \times 5 \times \cdots \times P + 1$, where P is a prime number. Each number N is formed by adding 1 to the product of some number of consecutive primes. Find a number N that is not a prime number.

B. What is the largest positive integer less than 1,000 that is the product of exactly three different primes?

C. Find the three smallest different primes whose sum is a prime number.

Copyright © 1982 by Dale Seymour Publications.

7. WARM-UP

Answers: A. $2 \times 3 \times 5 \times 7 \times 11 \times 13 + 1 =$
$30{,}031 = 59 \times 509$
B. $7 \times 2 \times 71 = 994$
C. $3 + 5 + 11 = 19$

Solution:

A. This process will always generate odd numbers. Inspection of each succeeding set of consecutive primes yields the following results.

$2 \times 3 + 1 = 7$ (prime)
$2 \times 3 \times 5 + 1 = 31$ (prime)
$2 \times 3 \times 5 \times 7 + 1 = 211$ (prime)
$2 \times 3 \times 5 \times 7 \times 11 + 1 = 2311$ (prime)
$2 \times 3 \times 5 \times 7 \times 11 \times 13 + 1 = 30{,}031 = 59 \times 509$

Thus, 30,031 is the smallest such N that is not prime.

B. Work backwards from 1000 and find the prime factors of each number.

$999 = 3 \times 3 \times 3 \times 37$ (four prime factors)
$998 = 2 \times 499$ (two prime factors)
997 is a prime number.
$996 = 2 \times 2 \times 3 \times 83$ (four prime factors)
$995 = 5 \times 199$ (two prime factors)
$994 = 2 \times 7 \times 71$ (three prime factors, all different)

Thus, 994 is the largest positive integer less than 1000 that is the product of exactly three different primes.

C. Make an organized listing of the sums of three different primes.

$2 + 3 + 5 = 10$
$2 + 3 + 7 = 12$
$2 + 3 + 11 = 16$
$2 + 3 + 13 = 18$
$2 + 3 + 17 = 22$

The sums of those triples beginning with 2 all are even numbers, and not prime.

$3 + 5 + 7 = 15$
$3 + 5 + 11 = 19$ (19 is prime.)

We have found one triple that produces a prime sum of 19. Are there any triples starting with 5 whose sum is prime?

$5 + 7 + 11 = 23$ (23 is prime.)

But 19 is less than 23, so the correct answer is $3 + 5 + 11 = 19$.

Teaching Suggestions:

These problems provide numerous opportunities for discussion of primes and factoring, and a quick review of many characteristics of prime numbers.

The solutions would be very tedious if the calculations were done by paper and pencil. By using the calculator as a problem-solving tool, students can concentrate on the procedures and patterns because the calculator enables them to make accurate calculations so rapidly.

Part A should stimulate a valuable discussion of the techniques of testing for primes. Suppose we admit 7 and 31 as obvious primes. The question then is whether 211 is prime. First, because we are determining prime factors, we need to consider only prime divisors. Second, we should determine the greatest prime divisor that needs to be tested, which is the greatest prime less than the square root of 211. The square root of 211 is approximately 14.525839, so the greatest prime divisor that must be tested is 13. For 2311, the square root is approximately 48.072861, so we need test only to 47. The greatest prime divisor to be tested on 30,031 is 173, but we strike gold at 59. By using the memory on a calculator, prime divisors can be determined in less than ten minutes.

Part C brings up interesting questions leading from the fact that any triple of primes starting with 2 produces an even sum. Some questions for discussion are, "What is the sum of two odd numbers? What is the sum of two even numbers? What is the sum of one odd and one even number? What is the sum of one even and two odd numbers? What is the sum of two even and one odd numbers? Does the quantity of even numbers affect a generalization? Does the quantity of odd numbers affect a generalization?" You might wish to generalize in terms of $2n$ and $2n - 1$.

In Part C we can eliminate a triple including the number 2, because it generates only even numbers, and all primes except 2 are odd numbers. Starting with 3, we quickly find $3 + 5 + 11$ to be a prime number. Our only remaining check is to determine if we could start a triple with 5 or 7 that would produce a sum less than or equal to 19. We illustrate that it cannot be done.

Antarian, Polarian, and Vegan played a game with three cards. Each card had a different positive whole number on it. The rules were as follows:

1. Deal one card to each player.
2. Score the number of points indicated on your card.
3. Shuffle the cards and deal again to play the next round.

They played at least two rounds. After the last round, Antarian had a total of 20 points, Polarian had 10 points, and Vegan had 9 points. During the last round of play, Polarian scored 8 points. How many rounds did they play? How many points did each player score in each round?

Copyright © 1982 by Dale Seymour Publications.

7. SCORE SUM

Answers: They played 3 rounds.

Distribution of points by rounds

	Antarian	Polarian	Vegan
Round 1	8	1	4
Round 2	8	1	4
Round 3	4	8	1
Totals:	20	10	9

Teaching Suggestions:

As often happens in mathematics, the key to this problem is to start at the end of the problem and work backwards. The critical point in the discussion of the problem is the significance of the total number of game points being 39. With some students you may need to ask what is known about the total number of points in each round. This is a desperation question, because the answer tends to open the problem for a quick solution.

Solution:

After the last round, the players have received a total of 39 points. Since the number of points scored in each round is constant, then 39 must equal the number of rounds multiplied by the points per round. $39 = 3 \times 13$ or 1×39. There is more than one round, so there must have been 3 rounds with 13 points distributed per round. Now we can set up a table and begin to determine the entries. Polarian's total score was 10 points, so he must have scored 1 point in each of the first two rounds.

	Antarian	Polarian	Vegan
Round 1		1	
Round 2		1	
Round 3		8	
Totals:	20	10	9

We know now that one of the cards shows 8, and one shows 1. Since the total number of points in one round is 13, the remaining card must show 4. Since Vegan has a total of 9 points, he could not have received 8 points in any round. So Antarian received 8 points in each of the first two rounds. The final distribution of points for Antarian to receive a total of 20 points and for Vegan to receive 9 points is

	Antarian	Polarian	Vegan
Round 1	8	1	4
Round 2	8	1	4
Round 3	4	8	1
Totals:	20	10	9

Consider the sets of integers that are in arithmetic progression with a constant difference of seven. That is, consider the sets of integers $7n - k$, where $k = 0, 1, 2, 3, 4, 5, 6$ and $n = 1, 2, 3, 4, \ldots$. For each value of k, list the first eight such consecutive integers. Now find the largest integer that will always divide the product of eight such consecutive integers, no matter what value of k is chosen.

Copyright © 1982 by Dale Seymour Publications.

7. EXTENSION

Answer: 5,760

Hint:

Write the numbers in each sequence in factored form.

Solution:

A "brute force" method involves writing out the product of each sequence of eight numbers in factored form, and then finding the greatest common divisor of all of the products. First, it is necessary to list each of the seven different sequences of eight numbers, and to factor each number. (You may wish to divide this task among groups of students.) A list of the products in factored form is shown below.

$7n - 0$: $2^7 \times 3^2 \times 5^1 \times 7^9$

$7n - 1$: $2^8 \times 3^5 \times 5^2 \times 11^1 \times 13^1 \times 17^1 \times 41^1$

(At this point, we can see that we only need to look for factors of 2, 3, and 5 in the products, because no larger factor can be common to $7n - 0$ and $7n - 1$.)

$7n - 2$: $2^8 \times 3^5 \times 5^2$

$7n - 3$: $2^{10} \times 3^3 \times 5^2$

$7n - 4$: $2^7 \times 3^4 \times 5^2$

$7n - 5$: $2^8 \times 3^5 \times 5^1$

$7n - 6$: $2^7 \times 3^3 \times 5^3$

By examination, the greatest common divisor is $2^7 \times 3^2 \times 5^1 = 5,760$.

Teaching Suggestions:

Encourage students to discuss all their observations about the patterns they see in this problem.

Have the students consider the units digits in each of the sequences. There is a repeating pattern . . . , 1, 8, 5, 2, 9, 6, 3, 0, 7, 4, ... Every fifth units digit is 5 or 0. So in some sequences, but not in all, two factors of 5 will occur.

Some students will notice patterns in the sequences of eight that lead them to a solution in the following way.

Alternate numbers in every sequence are even numbers. The pattern of their divisors is 2, 8, 2, 4, 2, 8, 2, 4, ... Thus, the product of every sequence of eight will have divisors of 2, 8, 2, and 4. Every third number in any sequence is divisible by 3. In some sequences, this means that only two numbers divisible by 3 will occur. Thus, in every sequence of eight there will always be at least two numbers divisible by 3, and so the product will be divisible by 3×3. Every fifth number in any sequence is divisible by 5, so the product of every sequence will be divisible by 5. The number 7 is a divisor only of the set 7, 14, 21, . . . , so it cannot be a divisor of the product of every sequence of eight. Hence, the greatest common divisor is $2 \times 8 \times 2 \times 4 \times 3 \times 3 \times 5 = 5,760$.

A. Complete the table below.

```
Row 1                    1
Row 2                  2   2
Row 3                3   4   3
Row 4              4   6   6   4
Row 5            5   8   9   8   5
Row 6          6  10  12  12  10   6
Row 7        7  12  15  16  15  12   7
Row 8      8  14  18  20  20  18  14   8
Row 9     __ __ __ __ __ __ __ __ __
Row 10   __ __ __ __ __ __ __ __ __ __
```

B. How many terms are in the 5th row? 8th row? 11th row? 16th row? *n*th row?

C. List the terms in the 15th row.

D. Write the set of numbers formed by the middle terms in the odd-numbered rows. Can you describe this set of numbers?

E. Find the absolute value of the difference in adjacent terms of the 10th row.

```
10   18   24   28   30   30   28   24   18   10
   8    6   __   __   __   __   __   __   __
```

F. Can you state a simple formula for calculating each term of the *n*th row?

Copyright © 1982 by Dale Seymour Publications.

Answers:
A. Row 9: 9, 16, 21, 24, 25, 24, 21, 16, 9
Row 10: 10, 18, 24, 28, 30, 30, 28, 24, 18, 10

B. 5; 8; 11; 16; n terms

C. Row 15: 15, 28, 39, 48, 55, 60, 63, 64, 63, 60, 55, 48, 39, 28, 15

D. 1, 4, 9, 16, 25, 36, . . .
The set of squares of positive whole numbers

E. 8, 6, 4, 2, 0, 2, 4, 6, 8

F. Row n: $n, 2n - 2, 3n - 6, 4n - 12,$

$5n - 20, 6n - 30, 7n - 42, . . . ,$
$2n - 2, n$

Hint:

Look for patterns in the rows and diagonals of the triangle.

Solution:

A. The table is a simple multiplication table arranged in a somewhat different manner. The first diagonal downward and to the left (or right) is the set of counting numbers, or multiples of 1. The second diagonal is the set of multiples of 2, and so on.

B. The number of terms in a row is the same as the row number. Thus, in the nth row there are n terms.

C. One could simply continue the pattern of multiples and write each of the rows 11 through 15 to produce an acceptable answer. Hopefully, students will look for patterns that produce simple formulas to generate row 15 without having to write all the preceding rows. The first term of any row is the same as the row number. So the first term in the 15th row is 15. The second term is a multiple of 2. However, these multiples of 2 start in row 2, so that the second term in row 15 is the 15 − 1 or 14th multiple of 2, or 2 × 14 = 28. The third term in row 15 is a multiple of 3, but it is the 15 − 2 or 13th multiple of 3, or 3 × 13 = 39. This pattern continues.

D. The elements in this set are 1, 4, 9, 16, ... Each is a perfect square, 1 × 1, 2 × 2, 3 × 3, and so on. Compare this set with the numbers on the diagonal (left to right) of a conventional multiplication table.

E. Note that the differences in row 10 are consecutive even numbers. In odd-numbered rows the differences are consecutive odd numbers.

F. Referring to the solution shown in part C above, the terms in the nth row will be n, $2(n − 1)$, $3(n − 2)$, $4(n − 3)$, $5(n − 4)$, $6(n − 5)$, . . . , $n(n − (n − 1))$ or $n(1)$ or n.

Teaching Suggestions:

As you begin the discussion of this problem, you may wish to relate the rotation of the square multiplication table to the triangular table shown in the problem.

$$
\begin{array}{ccccc}
1 & 2 & 3 & 4 & 5 & \cdots \\
2 & 4 & 6 & 8 & 10 & \cdots \\
3 & 6 & 9 & 12 & 15 & \cdots \\
4 & 8 & 12 & 16 & 20 & \cdots \\
5 & 10 & 15 & 20 & 25 & \cdots
\end{array}
$$

Note that in part E, if the differences are not defined as absolute values, the set formed will be a subset of successive odd numbers in odd-numbered rows,

Row 7: 7 12 15 16 15 12 7
    −5 −3 −1   1   3   5

successive even numbers in even-numbered rows,

Row 6: 6 10 12 12 10 6
    −4 −2   0   2   4

The subtraction of these differences left to right produces the constant difference of −2.

There are many relationships among the numbers in this triangle. For example, look at any diamond-shaped set of four numbers.

4 × 9 = 6 × 6   9 × 8 = 6 × 12

These patterns can also be related to the multiplication table.

This problem creates an infinite number of discussion possibilities. Use it to the fullest in the time you have available. One incentive can be to offer students extra credit for the discovery of additional patterns or formulas.

8. PAINT BY NUMBER

The counting numbers are arranged in five columns as shown below.

	A	B	C	D	E
Row 1	1	2	3	4	5
Row 2	9	8	7	6	
Row 3		10	11	12	13
Row 4	17	16	15	14	
Row 5		18	—	—	—
Row 6	—	—	—	—	
Row 7		—	—	—	—

Fill in the blanks to complete rows 5, 6, and 7. In which column and row will the number 1000 appear?

Copyright © 1982 by Dale Seymour Publications.

8. PAINT BY NUMBER

Answers: Row 5:   18 19 20 21
Row 6: 25 24 23 22
Row 7:   26 27 28 29

The number 1000 will fall in column B and row 250.

Hint:

Look for patterns in the columns.

Solution:

Column E has entries only in the odd-numbered rows. The entries in column E increase by 8 each time.

Row 1: $5 = 8 \times 1 - 3$
Row 3: $13 = 8 \times 2 - 3$
Row 5: $21 = 8 \times 3 - 3$
Row 7: $29 = 8 \times 4 - 3$

Which numbers in column E will help us find the position of 1000 on the chart? By trial and error, we find that $8 \times 125 - 3 = 997$. We can place 997 in column E and use the pattern in the chart to write out the rows until we reach 1000.

A	B	C	D	E
	994	995	996	997
1001	1000	999	998	

Thus, 1000 falls in column B.

To find the number of the row, look back at our list of elements in column E. Each element is just one more than a multiple of four.

$5 = 4 \times 1 + 1$
$13 = 4 \times 3 + 1$
$21 = 4 \times 5 + 1$
$29 = 4 \times 7 + 1$

And the multiple of four in each case is the same as the row number. So in the nth row, if n is odd, the element in column E equals $4 \times n + 1$. Now we can figure out which row 997 is in.

$997 = 4 \times n + 1$
$996 = 4 \times n$
$249 = n$

Since 1000 is in the next row down, it falls in row 250.

Teaching Suggestions:

This problem served the purpose of teaching the teacher. It was presented to me by a friend whose straightforward solution seemed obvious enough. I decided that any discussion might give away the solution, so I simply gave a due date, collected the students' papers, and in an offhand manner asked which column had been the key to the solution. My nonchalance disappeared rapidly when I found that *all* columns had been used. I was faced with the choice of suddenly becoming ill, necessitating a substitute, or thinking on my feet. Here are a few of the observations presented by my students.

a. Column C has a constant difference of 4. Thus, $4n - 1$ gives the correct entry in column C and the correct row number n.

b. The entries in column A differ by 8, and a formula similar to column E yields the correct entries in column A.

c. Columns B and D have interesting similarities. Where one increases by 2, the other increases by 6. In column B, $2(4n - 3)$ gives the odd-numbered row entries, and $2(4n)$ gives the even-numbered row entries. I leave column D to you.

d. If you draw a line under any row, the sums of the entries in columns B, C, and D will be equal.

e. Take a 3 by 3 block of numbers from columns B, C, and D. The sum of the diagonals are equal.

f. There were more. Had I observed all this? No! And, it was apparent to all concerned.

Moral of the story: If you are going to teach problem solving, then you had better solve the problem first and examine it for other possibilities. I was reminded again that to take a problem for granted is to put one foot (at least) in a bear trap.

There are three red flags, three blue flags, and three white flags. A signal is made by raising exactly three flags on a pole. Each flag may be raised into one of four vertical positions on the pole. All three flags may be the same color, or there may be just two of the same color, or all three may be different colors. How many different signals may be made under these conditions?

Examples of four different signals:

8. EXTENSION

Answer: 108 signals

Hint:

Make an organized listing of the signals and look for patterns.

Solution:

There are three color combinations to be considered.
   a. three flags of one color
   b. two flags of one color and one flag of another color
   c. three different-colored flags

a. Three red flags can be arranged in four ways: (r,r,r,_), (r,r,_,r), (r,_,r,r), (_,r,r,r). These arrangements are the same for the blue and the white flags. Thus, we have 4 × 3 = 12 signals.

b. There are six color combinations to consider: two red, one blue; two red, one white; two blue, one red; two blue, one white; two white, one red; and two white, one blue. We need to list the signals for just one color combination, such as two red, one blue, and then multiply by six.

   (r,r,b,_), (r,b,r,_), (b,r,r,_)
   (r,r,_,b), (r,b,_,r), (b,r,_,r)
   (r,_,r,b), (r,_,b,r), (b,_,r,r)
   (_,r,r,b), (_,r,b,r), (_,b,r,r)

There are 12 different signals for each of the 6 different color combinations, giving 12 × 6 = 72 possible signals. The important concept for young students is the observation that there are only three arrangements for the red, red, blue combination. The blank space creates four different placements of these three arrangements.

c. The three colors can be arranged in 6 different ways: (r,w,b), (r,b,w), (b,r,w), (b,w,r), (w,r,b), (w,b,r). The blank can be placed in 4 different locations in each of those arrangements, so we have 6 × 4 = 24 signals. Some students will want to list all the possible signals using three colors and a blank.

Adding the signals found in the three cases, we have 12 + 72 + 24 = 108 signals.

Teaching Suggestions:

Students will often take a haphazard approach to listing the arrangements in the beginning. The arrangements using all one color are somewhat obvious. The next step in the process, that of two-color, one-color arrangements, is where you may lend a helping hand. Students may start by considering one arrangement at a time, such as (r,_,b,r), then (r,r,b,_), and at each step checking to see that it differs from previous listings. You may at some point wish to provide the hint of finding all possible arrangements with the blank remaining stationary. This clues the student into the important observation in step (b) of the solution.

You might extend this problem by creating signals involving two flags as well as three flags. But be sure to work the problem yourself before assigning it.

Dolores asked Norman to measure the edges of a rectangular box and to leave the information on her desk. On returning she found that Norman had left her the areas of the faces of the box. Knowing that the edges each measured a whole number of inches, she determined the length, width, and height of the box. If the areas of the faces were 120, 96, and 80 square inches, find the lengths of the edges of the box. What is the volume of the box?

Copyright © 1982 by Dale Seymour Publications.

9. WARM-UP

Answers: The edges of the box are 8, 10, and 12 inches.

The volume is 960 cubic inches.

Solution:

In most cases, the students will take a trial-and-error approach. Beginning with 80, try different pairs of factors for 80 and see what happens to other two area numbers.

Areas of faces in square inches			
80	96	120	
1 × 80	1 × 96	80 × 96?	No.
2 × 40	2 × 48	40 × 48?	No.
4 × 20	4 × 24	20 × 24?	No.
5 × 16	16 × 6	5 × 6?	No.
8 × 10	8 × 12	10 × 12?	Yes!

Some students were able to shorten the trial-and-error method by looking at the prime factors of the three area numbers.

$$120 = 2^3 \times 3 \times 5$$
$$96 = 2^5 \times 3$$
$$80 = 2^4 \times 5$$

They observed that 2^3 was common to all three numbers. The area of 80 square inches would then be 8 × 10. The area of 120 might be 8 × 15 or 10 × 12. Because 12 is a common factor of both 96 and 120, the students determined the lengths of the edges to be 8, 10, and 12 inches.

Once the lengths of the edges are known, the volume is found by taking the product of those lengths 8 × 10 × 12 = 960 cubic inches.

Teaching Suggestions:

You may wish to set up the table shown in the solution to help students organize their trial-and-error approach. The table will lead them to seek information regarding the divisors of the three area numbers.

A more lengthy discussion might concern the means of determining the number of divisors of a given number. If the prime factors of a given number are p^a, q^b, r^c, and so on, where p, q, and r are prime numbers and a, b, and c represent the number of times each prime factor occurs, then the number of divisors is $(a + 1)(b + 1)(c + 1), \ldots$. Thus, for $80 = 2^4 \times 5^1$, then the number of divisors is $(4 + 1)(1 + 1) = 5 \times 2 = 10$. The divisors of 80 are 1, 2, 4, 5, 8, 10, 16, 20, 40, 80.

There are many ways of arranging the digits 1 through 9 in a 3 by 3 square array. Using each digit only once, can you arrange them so that the three-digit numbers in the horizontal rows are all perfect squares?

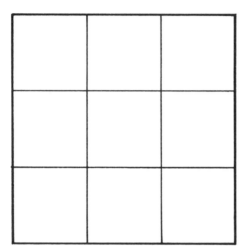

Copyright © 1982 by Dale Seymour Publications.

9. PERFECT PLUNGE

Answer:

3	6	1
7	8	4
5	2	9

or any similar arrangement of the numbers such as

7	8	4
3	6	1
5	2	9

Hint:

Use a calculator to make a list of all the three-digit perfect squares.

Solution:

The only perfect squares with three different digits are 169, 196, 256, 289, 324, 361, 529, 576, 625, 729, 784, 841, and 961. Finding these is a simple calculator project. Finding the solution is a more difficult chore. To avoid lengthy trial and error, let us apply a little logical thinking to the problem. The digit 3 occurs with the least frequency in our list. So the solution must include either 324 or 361.

Suppose we start with 324. Then we reduce our eligible list to numbers containing 1, 5, 6, 7, 8, and 9. They are 169, 196, 576, and 961. But all of these numbers contain a 6, so it is not possible to choose from this reduced list two other three-digit numbers using each digit only once.

So 361 is our only remaining possibility. We reduce our eligible list to numbers containing 2, 4, 5, 7, 8, and 9. They are 289, 529, 729, and 784. The only number containing a 4 is 784. We now have two numbers for our solution, 361 and 784. This reduces our list to numbers containing 2, 5, and 9. The only such perfect square is 529. Thus, we have for our solution the numbers 361, 784, and 529.

Teaching Suggestions:

Here is another place to demonstrate the power of the calculator. Students can usually generate the list of perfect squares with three different digits in less than three minutes.

One pertinent question that may need to be asked of your students is where to start. What number(s) might be the best choice? If you ask this question, don't let them answer it aloud.

Once you have completed the discussion of how the three numbers were determined, you might want to extend the problem. In how many ways can you arrange the three numbers in the rows of the square array? Do any of these arrangements produce a perfect square number reading downward by columns? The six possible arrangements are shown below.

361	361	784	784	529	529
784	529	361	529	784	361
529	784	529	361	361	784

Each number reading downward will contain three different digits, so that the list of perfect squares generated in the solution of the original problem can be used to check against. Examination of the six sets shows that none of the numbers in the columns are perfect squares.

9. EXTENSION

The *natural numbers* are the numbers 1, 2, 3, 4, 5, 6, ... Use the table below to record your answers to the following questions.

A. Find the cubes of the natural numbers.

B. Find the sums of the cubes.

C. Find the square root of each of those sums.

D. Write a formula that expresses the sum of n consecutive cubes.

Number n	Cube n^3	Sum of cubes $S(n^3)$	Square root of sum of cubes $\sqrt{S(n^3)}$
1	$1^3 = 1$	$1 = 1$	$\sqrt{1} = 1$
2	$2^3 = 8$	$1+8 = 9$	$\sqrt{9} = 3$
3	$3^3 = 27$	$1+8+27 = 36$	$\sqrt{36} = 6$
4			
5			
6			
7			
8			
9			
10			
•			
•			
•			
15			
•			
•			
•			
20			
•			
•			
•			
n			

Copyright © 1982 by Dale Seymour Publications.

9. EXTENSION

Answer:

n	n^3	$S(n^3)$	$\sqrt{S(n^3)}$
1	1	1	1
2	8	9	3
3	27	36	6
4	64	100	10
5	125	225	15
6	216	441	21
7	343	784	28
8	512	1,296	36
9	729	2,025	45
10	1,000	3,025	55
.	.	.	.
.	.	.	.
.	.	.	.
15	3,375	14,400	120
.	.	.	.
.	.	.	.
.	.	.	.
20	8,000	44,100	210
.	.	.	.
.	.	.	.
.	.	.	.
n	n^3	$\left(\dfrac{n(n+1)}{2}\right)^2$	$\dfrac{n(n+1)}{2}$

Hint:

Use a calculator to compute some entries, but be alert for patterns that will help you find the other entries more efficiently.

Solution:

The column n^3 can be easily determined by a calculator.

The sums of the cubes can be seen as a set of perfect square numbers. Upon examination of these perfect squares, they are found to be the squares of the set of triangular numbers 1, 3, 6, 10, 15, ... (See problem 15. *Warm-up* for more on triangular numbers.) Since the nth triangular number is $\dfrac{n(n+1)}{2}$, the sum of the first n consecutive cubes is $\left(\dfrac{n(n+1)}{2}\right)^2$.

Teaching Suggestions:

One purpose of keeping a notebook in mathematics is to be able to look back and find similar patterns or situations. Most students will remember encountering the set of triangular numbers before. The use of the formula makes the completion of the table a simple task. A few students will work out all the numerical entries in the table. This is a correct process, but you should encourage students to look for the pattern and to "re-discover" its formula.

Interesting little extension problems or discussions can spring from this problem. One example is: If the cubes of the first 43 natural numbers are added, what is the last digit in the sum? (6)

Maria has four math books, three novels, and two books of poetry. She wants to arrange them on her shelf so that all the math books are together on the left end of the shelf, all the novels are together in the middle, and the books of poetry are together on the right end. How many different arrangements of the books are possible?

Copyright © 1982 by Dale Seymour Publications.

Answer: 288 arrangements

Hint:

In how many possible ways can she arrange just the math books? Just the novels? Just the poetry books?

Solution:

Many students will need to picture the arrangements, either in a tree diagram or in an organized listing.

Suppose the math books are designated A, B, C, and D. A partial tree diagram of the 24 possible arrangements is shown below.

There are 6 arrangements beginning with A, 6 more with B, and 6 more with each of C and D, making 4 × 6 = 24 arrangements.

Another way to think about the arrangements of the math books is to visualize the four places the books could occupy on the shelf, and to consider the number of choices for each place. There are 4 different books that can occupy the first place. Then for the second place there are 3 books left to choose from. Similarly, there are 2 choices for the third place, and only 1 for the last place.

4	3	2	1

The product 4 × 3 × 2 × 1 = 24 yields the total number of arrangements.

Following the same reasoning, the three novels can be arranged in 3 × 2 × 1 = 6 different ways. The two books of poetry can be arranged in 2 × 1 = 2 different ways.

Now we must consider the arrangements of all nine books on the shelf. Each of the 24 arrangements of math books can be followed by 6 arrangements of the novels, which can in turn be followed by 2 arrangements of the books of poetry. So there are 24 × 6 × 2 = 288 possible arrangements.

Teaching Suggestions:

Even after finding the 24, 6, and 2 arrangements of the three groups of books, students may not readily see the linkage of 24 arrangements, each followed by 6 arrangements, each followed by 2 arrangements, giving a total of 288 arrangements. It may be necessary for students to picture a simpler problem in order to understand this kind of linkage. Ask them to picture the problem using only two books in each set. A partial tree diagram is shown below for the groups of books (a,b), (c,d), and (e,f).

An extension to this problem is to find the possible arrangements if the three groups of books can be rearranged along the shelf. Since the three sets of books can be arranged in 6 different ways (math, novels, poetry; novels, math, poetry; etc.) there are 6 × 288 = 1728 ways to arrange all the books.

How many different six-digit numbers can you make using the digits 1, 2, 5, 6, 7, and 9? How many of these six-digit numbers are divisible by six?

Copyright © 1982 by Dale Seymour Publications.

Answers: There are 720 possible arrangements.
240 of these numbers are divisible by six.

Hints:

Make a tree diagram or an organized listing.

How can you tell if a number is divisible by six?

Solution:

My students seem to gain the greatest understanding of a problem when they can picture the solution. Therefore, I find drawing tree diagrams to be invaluable to this age group.

If 1 is the left-hand digit, there are 24 ways × 5 = 120 arrangements. So if we start the tree with the digit 2, there will be a similar counting pattern yielding 120 number arrangements. Since we have 6 possibilities for the left-hand digit, each producing 120 number arrangements, we have a total of 6 × 120 = 720 possible arrangements.

To be divisible by 6, a number must be divisible by both 2 and 3. The sum of the digits 1 + 2 + 5 + 6 + 7 + 9 = 30, which is divisible by 3. Hence all of the 720 different six-digit numbers are divisible by 3. Only the numbers ending in an even digit, here 2 or 6, can be divisible by 2. In our set of numbers, two out of every six numbers will be divisible by 2, or one-third of the 720 numbers, or 240 numbers.

Teaching Suggestions:

Students need a great deal of practice in developing counting concepts and in picturing solutions. I always urge teachers *not* to give students a quick formula. The use of a formula is a memory fact and eliminates the understanding developed by a picture. I do many problems involving counting with tree diagrams. A few very bright youngsters develop a formula for themselves. That is great. I never discourage this, but the majority of my students need to *see* the solution. They will be ready for the formula approach on reaching a structured probability unit in the second-year Algebra course, and it will be a meaningful formula to them.

This is an opportunity to review simple divisibility rules. The simplicity of the second part of this problem lies in the recognition that all 720 number arrangements are divisible by 3.

A *palindromic number* is one that reads the same from left to right or from right to left. An example is 46764. How many palindromic numbers are there between 10 and 100,000?

Answer: 1089 palindromes

Hint:

How many two-digit palindromes are there? How many three-digit? Four-digit? Five-digit?

Solution:

In a two-digit palindromic number, both digits must be the same. There are 9 such palindromic numbers, 11, 22, 33, . . . , 99.

In a three-digit palindrome, the first and third digits must be the same. There are 9 ways in which this can happen, 1 _ 1, 2 _ 2, . . . , 9 _ 9. For the middle digit, any of the 10 digits from 0 through 9 may be used. Thus we have $9 \times 10 = 90$ three-digit palindromes.

In a four-digit palindrome, the first and fourth digits must be the same, and the two middle digits must be the same. There are 9 ways to make the first and last digits equal, 1 _ _ 1, 2 _ _ 2, . . . , 9 _ _ 9. For each of those ways, the middle digits must be one of the 10 combinations 00, 11, 22, . . . , 99. Thus, there are $9 \times 10 = 90$ four-digit palindromic numbers.

In a five-digit palindrome, again the first and last digits must be the same. There are 9 possibilities, 1 _ _ _ 1, 2 _ _ _ 2, . . . , 9 _ _ _ 9. The second and fourth digits must also be the same. There are 10 ways for this to happen, 0 _ 0, 1 _ 1, 2 _ 2, . . . , 9 _ 9. The middle digit may be any of the 10 digits 0 through 9. Thus, we have $9 \times 10 \times 10 = 900$ possible five-digit palindromic numbers.

In all, there are $9 + 90 + 90 + 900 = 1089$ palindromic numbers between 10 and 100,000.

Teaching Suggestions:

Be sure that the students clearly understand the meaning of palindrome. You can help clarify this through the use of palindromic words such as RADAR, MADAM, and palindromic phrases such as YREKA BAKERY.

Many observations can result from this problem. For example, the number of palindromes between 100 and 1000 is 90. Between 1000 and 10,000 it is again 90. From 10,000 to 100,000 the number of palindromes is 900. From 100,000 to 1,000,000 the number of palindromes will again be 900. What happens to numbers greater than 1,000,000?

There are many related problems involving palindromic numbers. Here is one well suited to using a calculator.

Given a three-digit non-palindromic number, reverse the digits and add. Continue the process to see if you will arrive at a palindromic number. Does this process always produce palindromes?

Example: 462 (Not a palindrome.)
           264

           726 (Not a palindrome.)
           627

           1353 (Not a palindrome.)
           3531

           4884 (Eureka! A palindrome.)

Here are three different views of one cube.

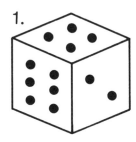
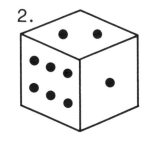
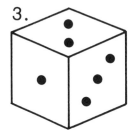

The same cube is shown again below, but some of the faces have been left blank. How many dots should there be on each of the blank faces?

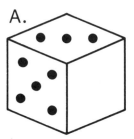
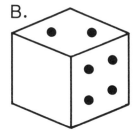
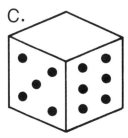

Copyright © 1982 by Dale Seymour Publications.

11. WARM-UP

Answers: A. 4 dots
B. 3 dots
C. 4 dots

Hint:

Make a model of the cube.

Solution:

This problem involves perceptual skills as well as logical reasoning. Students may want to make a model of the cube, recording the information presented in the three different views of the cube. Using a model will help them to be able to understand the relationships that are pictured in the problem.

On a more abstract level, students may work from the pictures alone to see such relationships as

1 dot and 4 dots are on opposite faces.
3 dots and 6 dots are on opposite faces.
So 5 dots must be opposite 2 dots.

Then for part A, we know that 6 dots will be hidden (opposite 3 dots) and 2 dots will be hidden (opposite 5 dots). The face showing must have either 1 dot or 4 dots. Look at view 3 of the cube. If it is rotated around the 1-dot face, and then turned one-quarter clockwise on its base, the cube will be in the position shown in part A. Hence the 1-dot face will be hidden and the 4-dot face will show.

Part B is easier to visualize. In view 1 of the cube, we see that the 6-dot face joins with the 2-dot and 4-dot faces at a vertex of the cube. Hence the 3-dot face must also join with the 2-dot and 4-dot faces, and will be seen on the cube shown in part B.

For part C, we can refer to view 1 of the cube. Mentally turn view 1 counterclockwise one-quarter on its base until it looks like part C. Then the 4-dot face will still be showing in part C.

Teaching Suggestions:

Any rectangular box or blank cube can serve as a model for students to use.

There are many different ways to solve these problems. Encourage your students to discuss all of their approaches, so that other students may learn new ways of thinking about this type of visual perception problem.

The design of a soccer ball is based on a solid figure called a *truncated icosahedron* Three different views of this solid are shown below.

How many black pentagons does the solid have?
How many white hexagons does the solid have?

Copyright © 1982 by Dale Seymour Publications.

11. PELE'S DELIGHT

Answers: 12 black pentagons

20 white hexagons

Solution:

This is a problem requiring good visual thinking and logical reasoning.

One way to count the shapes is to think of the solid as a globe, with a black pentagon at the north pole. Surrounding this are five white hexagons, then five more pentagons. The arrangement is the same around the black pentagon at the south pole. Along the equator are five white hexagons.

There are six pentagons in each hemisphere, or a total of 12.

There are five hexagons in each hemisphere, plus five along each side of the equator, or a total of 20.

Teaching Suggestions:

You may want to bring a soccer ball into class to use as a model.

Some students may enjoy learning about more of the different kinds of polyhedra that have been classified by mathematicians. A good resource is *Polyhedron Models* by Magnus J. Wenninger, published in 1971 by Cambridge University Press.

Three different views of the same solid figure are shown below.

A. How many triangles are on the figure? How many pentagons? How many squares?

B. How many triangle edges are there on the figure?

C. How many edges are there altogether on the figure?

Copyright © 1982 by Dale Seymour Publications.

11. EXTENSION

Answers: A. There are 20 triangles, 12 pentagons, and 30 squares.

B. 60 triangle edges

C. 120 edges altogether

Solution:

A. Suppose the solid is viewed as a globe, with a pentagon at each pole. Then in each hemisphere there are six pentagons, or a total of 12.

Each pentagon is surrounded by five squares. If we multiply the number of pentagons by the number of surrounding squares, we have $12 \times 5 = 60$. But since each square touches two pentagons, we have counted each square twice. Hence, there must be $60 \div 2 = 30$ squares.

Each pentagon touches the vertices of five triangles. So the number of pentagons times the number of touching triangles is $12 \times 5 = 60$. But each triangle touches three pentagons, so we have counted each triangle three times. Hence, there must be $60 \div 3 = 20$ triangles.

B. Each triangle has three edges, so there are $3 \times 20 = 60$ triangle edges on the solid figure.

C. We need to count the edges that are not triangle edges, that is, the edges formed by a pentagon and a square meeting. There are five such edges around each of the pentagons, or $5 \times 12 = 60$ edges. Thus, there are 120 edges altogether on the figure.

Teaching Suggestions:

Encourage the students to discuss the different ways they solved this problem. Solving such visual perception problems takes practice, but students can learn valuable techniques by listening to each other's reasoning.

This solid is called a *rhombicosidodecahedron*.

A. Given a three-liter unmarked container, a five-liter unmarked container, and an unlimited supply of water, can you obtain an accurate measure of four liters of water? You may pour from container to container or back into your water supply. Record your results in the tables.

5-liter	3 liter
0	0
0	3

5-liter	3 liter
0	0
5	0

B. On the pool table shown below, a pool ball must be shot initially from the point (0,0) and must roll along the cushion to either (0,3) or (5,0). Each time the ball strikes another cushion, it will bounce off at an angle of 60° as indicated by the dotted lines. First, start at (0,0), shoot the ball toward (5,0), and record the coordinates each time the ball strikes a cushion. Then start at (0,0), shoot the ball toward (0,3), and record the coordinates again. Can you relate your results to the tables in part A?

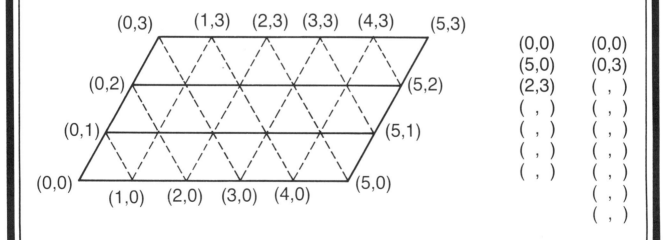

(0,0)   (0,0)
(5,0)   (0,3)
(2,3)   (,)
(,)   (,)
(,)   (,)
(,)   (,)
(,)   (,)
         (,)
         (,)

Copyright © 1982 by Dale Seymour Publications.

Answers: A.

5-liter	3-liter
0	0
0	3
3	0
3	3
5	1
0	1
1	0
1	3
④	0

5-liter	3-liter
0	0
5	0
2	3
2	0
0	2
5	2
④	3

B.

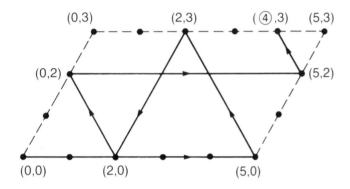

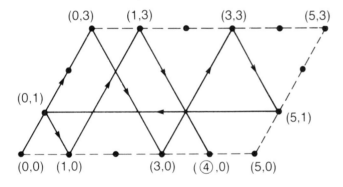

The lists of coordinates are the same as the lists of pourings in part A.

Solution:

A. Most students will need to experiment with different pourings for a while before they come upon a successful sequence. You may want to have the students compare their pouring sequences to determine which ones are the most efficient. Any correct sequence of pourings is an acceptable solution. The sequences shown in the answers are the most efficient ones. The minimum number of pourings required is six.

B. Notice that the list of coordinates for the bouncing ball is the same as the sequence of pourings necessary to achieve the four-liter measure. This "pool table" model will come in handy in solving *Splish Splash* and its *Extension*.

Teaching Suggestions:

Be sure that the students understand the directions for pouring. You may need to clarify that water may be poured from one container to another, either to fill the one container, or to empty the other. Also, all of the contents of one container may be poured back into the water source.

You may need to explain the method of recording the pouring sequence. The numbers in each row of the table refer to the amount of water present in each of the two containers. The pouring and filling needed to achieve each step is inferred from the amounts shown in the row.

This is a good problem to be used in conjunction with introducing the coordinate plane. I use the concept of *x*-axis and *y*-axis in discussing the development of the pool table model.

Notice that if a wrong 60° turn is executed on the model, it will place you into a repeating pattern. As a result, you will not find the minimum number of pourings required to achieve the desired capacity.

Given a four-liter unmarked container, a seven-liter unmarked container, and an unlimited supply of water, can you obtain an accurate measure of five liters of water? If so, what is the minimum number of pourings necessary?

Copyright © 1982 by Dale Seymour Publications.

12. SPLISH SPLASH

Answer: Two correct sequences of pourings are

(0,0)	(0,0)
(0,4)	(7,0)
(4,0)	(3,4)
(4,4)	(3,0)
(7,1)	(0,3)
(0,1)	(7,3)
(1,0)	(6,4)
(1,4)	(6,0)
(⑤,0)	(2,4)
	(2,0)
	(0,2)
	(7,2)
	(⑤,4)

The minimum number of pourings is 8.

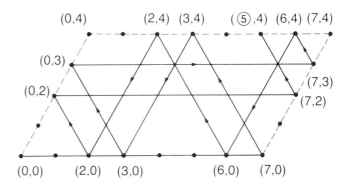

Solution:

A correct sequence of pourings can be determined by trial and error. But hopefully, the students will recall the "pool table" model used in problem *12. Warm-up,* and apply it to the solution of this problem.

The first step is to set up the coordinate system on the model. Since the two containers hold four liters and seven liters, the sides of the model must be four units and seven units long. The students will need to follow the bouncing ball twice, starting along each of the sides of the table.

Teaching Suggestions:

Students can demonstrate their understanding of coordinates by correctly listing the coordinates around the pool table model. Then they can follow the bouncing ball and quickly determine a solution.

It appears that following the shorter route on the first bounce determines the minimum number of pourings.

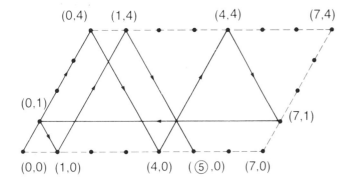

A. Given a five-liter unmarked container, a nine-liter unmarked container, and an unlimited supply of water, can you obtain an accurate measure of six liters of water? If so, what is the minimum number of pourings necessary?

B. Under the same conditions, but with a three-liter container and a six-liter container, can you obtain a measure of five liters? If so, what is the minimum number of pourings necessary?

Copyright © 1982 by Dale Seymour Publications.

12. EXTENSION

Answers: A. Two correct sequences of pourings are

(0,0)	(0,0)
(0,5)	(9,0)
(5,0)	(4,5)
(5,5)	(4,0)
(9,1)	(0,4)
(0,1)	(9,4)
(1,0)	(8,5)
(1,5)	(8,0)
(⑥,0)	(3,5)
	(3,0)
	(0,3)
	(9,3)
	(7,5)
	(7,0)
	(2,5)
	(2,0)
	(0,2)
	(9,2)
	(⑥,5)

The minimum number of pourings is 8.

B. It is not possible to obtain a measure of five liters.

Solution:

Once again, the pool table model enables students to quickly find solutions.

A.

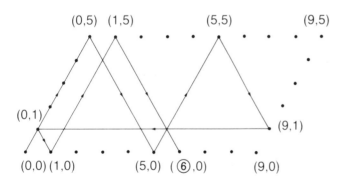

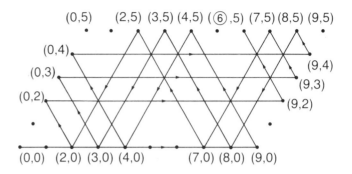

B. The three-liter and six-liter problem has no solution. Notice that you continually retrace a path, and that no 60° turn will allow you to reach any set of coordinates except those containing multiples of three.

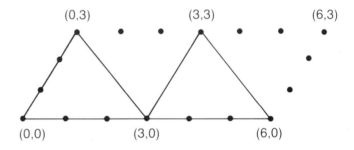

Teaching Suggestions:

You may wish to have your students explore further which measures can be used for the liter containers so that there will be a solution. One conjecture is that the two containers must have measures that are relatively prime.

Dinah is holding four cards, an ace of clubs, an ace of diamonds, an ace of hearts, and an ace of spades. Alice draws two of the cards. What is the probability that Alice will draw at least one red ace?

Copyright © 1982 by Dale Seymour Publications.

13. WARM-UP

Answer: 5/6

Hint:

Draw a tree diagram to show all the possible ways Alice can draw two cards.

Solution:

Most students need to see all the possibilities pictured.

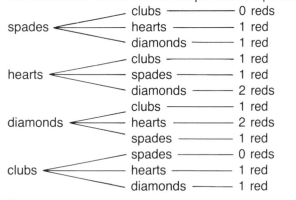

spades — clubs ———— 0 reds
— hearts ———— 1 red
— diamonds ——— 1 red

hearts — clubs ———— 1 red
— spades ———— 1 red
— diamonds ——— 2 reds

diamonds — clubs ———— 1 red
— hearts ———— 2 reds
— spades ———— 1 red

clubs — spades ———— 0 reds
— hearts ———— 1 red
— diamonds ——— 1 red

There are 12 different pairs of cards that Alice can draw. Of these, 10 pairs have at least one red ace in them. So the probability of Alice drawing at least one red ace is 10/12 or 5/6.

Teaching Suggestions:

This problem is a good one because virtually every student guesses that the probability is 1/2, until taking the time to picture the problem with a tree diagram.

Some students analyzed correctly that each ace could be paired with one of three remaining aces. Thus, there are 4×3 or 12 possible pairs. Only two possibilities exist to draw both black aces, the ace of clubs first and then the ace of spades, or the reverse order. So the probability of *not* drawing any red aces is 2/12. Thus the probability of drawing at least one red ace is $1 - 2/12 = 10/12$ or 5/6.

Play a game with five cards numbered 1, 2, 3, 4, and 5. Shuffle the cards, call the number "one," and turn over the first card. Then call "two" and turn over the second card. Continue counting aloud and turning the cards over. What is the probability that *none* of your calls will match the number on the card you turn over?

Copyright © 1982 by Dale Seymour Publications.

13. CARD SHARK

Answer: The probability is 44/120 or 11/30.

Hint:

Make a tree diagram of the ways in which the cards can be arranged.

Solution:

First we assume that the first card turned over is a 1. We know that there is a match already, so that the chance of not having a match will be 0 out of however many possible arrangements there are. But we need to make the tree to find out the number of possible arrangements.

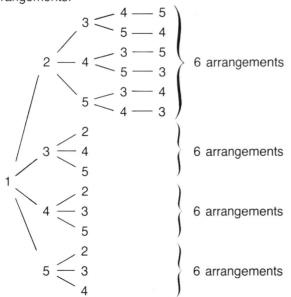

There are 24 possible arrangements, so the probability of not having a match is 0/24 or 0.

Suppose that the first card turned over is a 2. Every branch of the tree diagram below in which there is no match is marked with an asterisk.

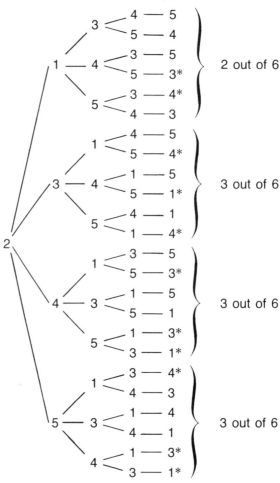

There are 24 arrangements, and 11 cases in which there is no match. So the probability of not having a match is 11/24.

Students should begin to find some shortcuts to making the tree diagrams that begin with 3, 4, and 5 as the first cards. In each tree diagram they should find 24 arrangements, and 11 cases of no matches. In all, there are 5 × 24 = 120 possible arrangements and 4 × 11 = 44 cases in which there is no match. So the probability that none of the calls will match the cards turned over is 44/120, or 11/30.

Teaching Suggestions:

Students must be very careful in setting up the tree diagrams in this problem. You might allow them to work in pairs so that they can check each other's diagrams and counting of the non-matches.

Five tickets are sold for a raffle. You buy three of the five raffle tickets. Two of the tickets are to be drawn as winning tickets. What is the probability of your *not* having a winning ticket drawn? What is the probability of your having *one* winning ticket drawn? What is the probability of your having *two* winning tickets drawn?

Copyright © 1982 by Dale Seymour Publications.

Answers: The probability of no winning ticket is 1/10.

The probability of one winning ticket is 6/10 or 3/5.

The probability of two winning tickets is 3/10.

Hint:

Make a tree diagram or an organized listing of the ways in which the two winning tickets can be drawn.

Solution:

Suppose that we identify the tickets we purchased by A, B, C and the other two raffle tickets by X, Y. Below is a partial tree diagram and a complete organized listing of the ways in which the two tickets can be drawn.

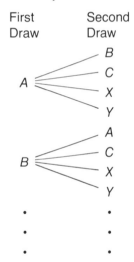

First Draw   Second Draw

AB, AC, AX, AY
BA, BC, BX, BY
CA, CB, CX, CY
XA, XB, XC, XY
YA, YB, YC, YX

There are 5 × 4 = 20 possible ways that the two winning tickets can be drawn. By examining the organized listing, we can count the number of pairs in which we have zero, one, or two winning tickets.

The only pairs that do not contain any of our tickets are XY and YX. So the probability of not having a winning ticket drawn is 2/20 or 1/10.

There are 6 pairs in which we have both tickets: AB, AC, BA, BC, CA, CB. So the probability of having two winning tickets drawn is 6/20 or 3/10.

There are 12 pairs that contain exactly one of our tickets, so the probability of having one winning ticket drawn is 12/20 or 6/10 or 3/5. Some students will count all 12 pairs, some will subtract 6 + 2 from 20, while others will recall that the maximum probability is 1, and 1 − 1/10 − 3/10 = 6/10.

Teaching Suggestions:

I find that a "feeling" for probability develops slowly for junior high students. If they arrive at the point where they can quickly picture somewhat elementary probability problems, you may wish to carry them a step further in their development.

For example, let us consider this solution from a different point of view. This situation involves two draws, and on each draw there will be a certain number of tickets to choose from. The total sample space, or total number of different pairs of tickets that can be drawn is

$\underset{\text{1st draw}}{\underline{5 \text{ choices}}} \times \underset{\text{2nd draw}}{\underline{4 \text{ choices}}} = 20$ possible pairs.

We have purchased three tickets, and the number of ways in which two of our tickets can be drawn is

$\underset{\text{1st draw}}{\underline{3 \text{ choices}}} \times \underset{\text{2nd draw}}{\underline{2 \text{ choices}}} = 6$ ways, yielding a probability of 6/20 or 3/10.

There are only two tickets that we don't have, and the number of ways in which both of those tickets can be drawn (giving us no winning tickets) is

$\underset{\text{1st draw}}{\underline{2 \text{ choices}}} \times \underset{\text{2nd draw}}{\underline{1 \text{ choice}}} = 2$ ways, yielding a probability of 2/20 or 1/10.

Perhaps the simplest way to think about the probability of having just one winning ticket is to remember that the total probability in this problem is 1, and that P(no winning ticket) + P(two winning tickets) + P(one winning ticket) = 1. So the probability of having one winning ticket is 1 − 3/10 − 1/10 = 6/10.

Suppose that you and a friend are playing a game with two dice. One die is numbered 0, 1, 2, 3, 4, 5 and the other is numbered 1, 2, 3, 4, 5, 6. You and your friend take turns rolling both dice and scoring the number of points rolled. The winner of the game will be the player whose score is closest to 21. After two rolls of the dice your score is 18 points. If you choose to roll the dice one more time, what is the probability of maintaining or improving your score?

Copyright © 1982 by Dale Seymour Publications.

Answer: 7/12

Hints:

What numbers can you roll that will maintain or improve your score?

Make a tree diagram of the possible ways the two dice can be throw.

Solution:

The only scores that are equal to or better than 18 are 19, 20, 21, 22, 23, and 24. So any throw between one and six inclusive will either maintain or improve the score. The 36 possibilities are shown by tree diagrams. Each score between one and six is marked with an asterisk.

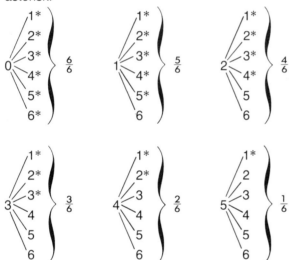

Thus, the probability of maintaining or improving the score is 6 + 5 + 4 + 3 + 2 + 1 = 21 ways out of 36 possibilities, or 21/36 or 7/12.

Teaching Suggestions:

As you begin to provide ample opportunities for students to get a feeling for probability, it is important to have them first make educated guesses about each situation. Questions such as, "Would you throw or not throw in this situation?" should be considered before any work is done on the solution.

Some students will quickly see patterns and be able to verbalize them without drawing all the trees. These students are close to developing a formula on their own. This is exactly what we want to have happening.

From a hat containing 20 consecutively numbered tickets, two tickets are drawn at random without replacement. If the smaller number is subtracted from the larger, what is the probability that the difference of the two numbers is ten or less than ten?

Copyright © 1982 by Dale Seymour Publications.

14. HAT TRICK

Answers: 290/380 or 29/38

Hints:

How many different pairs of tickets can be drawn?

Make an organized listing of the pairs whose difference is ten or less.

Solution:

There are 20 lottery tickets, numbered 1 through 20. On the first draw, there are 20 possible choices. With each of those choices, there are 19 possible choices on the second draw. Thus there are $20 \times 19 = 380$ possible pairs of tickets that can be drawn.

Now we list the pairs whose difference is ten or less, and look for patterns.

First Draw	Second Draw	Number of Pairs
20	10, 11, . . . , 19	10
19	9, 10, . . . , 18, 20	11
18	8, . . . , 17, 19, 20	12
17	7, . . . , 16, 18, 19, 20	13
16	6, . . . , 15, 17, . . . , 20	14
15	5, . . . , 14, 16, . . . , 20	15
14	4, . . . , 13, 15, . . . , 20	16
13	3, . . . , 12, 14, . . . , 20	17
12	2, . . . , 11, 13, . . . , 20	18
11	1, . . . , 10, 12, . . . , 20	19
10	1, . . . , 9, 11, . . . , 20	19
9	1, . . . , 8, 10, . . . , 19	18
8	1, . . . , 7, 9, . . . , 18	17
7	1, . . . , 6, 8, . . . , 17	16
6	. . . .	15
5	. . . .	14
4	. . . .	13
3	. . . .	12
2	. . . .	11
1	. . . .	10

The total number of pairs with a difference of ten or less is $2(10 + 11 + . . . + 19) = 290$. Thus, the probability of drawing two tickets whose numbers have a difference of ten or less is 290/380 or 29/38.

Teaching Suggestions:

Be sure that the students understand that they are to find the absolute value of the difference between the two ticket numbers.

Encourage them to look for patterns that will shorten their listing work.

Finding the sum $10 + 11 + . . . + 19$ gives another opportunity for students to use Gauss' technique for finding such sums.

$$10 + 11 + 12 + 13 + 14 + 15 + 16 + 17 + 18 + 19$$

5 pairs, each with a sum of 29.
$5 \times 29 = 195$

A container holds six red marbles and four green marbles. You select two marbles from the container (without replacement). What is the probability that you will select one red marble and one green marble?

Copyright © 1982 by Dale Seymour Publications.

14. EXTENSION

Answer: 8/15

Solution:

Each of the red marbles can be drawn, followed by five other possible red marbles. To keep track of the different red marbles, number them R_1, R_2, R_3, R_4, R_5, R_6. Thus, R_1 could be paired with each of the other red marbles to make five pairs: R_1R_2, R_1R_3, R_1R_4, R_1R_5, R_1R_6. These pairs could be drawn with six possible starting marbles, R_1 through R_6. So there are $6 \times 5 = 30$ possible pairs of two red marbles.

Each of the green marbles G_1, G_2, G_3, G_4 can be paired in a similar fashion with three other green marbles, giving $4 \times 3 = 12$ possible pairs of two green marbles.

Each of the six red marbles can be paired with any of the four different green marbles to make $6 \times 4 = 24$ pairs of marbles drawn red, then green.

Each of the four green marbles can be drawn followed by any of the six different red marbles to make $4 \times 6 = 24$ pairs of marbles drawn green, then red.

We now have $30 + 12 + 24 + 24 = 90$ possible pairings. Of these, $24 + 24 = 48$ are pairs in which one marble is red and the other is green. Thus, the probability of drawing one red and one green marble is 48/90 or 8/15.

Teaching Suggestions:

The phrase "without replacement" indicates that during the drawing of two marbles, the first marble is to be drawn and kept out of the container while the second marble is being drawn. Then both marbles are returned to the container before the next drawing takes place.

With younger students, do not read R_1 or G_2 in subscript language as "R sub 1," or "G sub 2." So that students get a better understanding of this notation, always refer to them as "the first red marble" (R_1), "the second green marble" (G_2), and so on.

The solution can also be demonstrated with a tree diagram, and many students will choose this method.

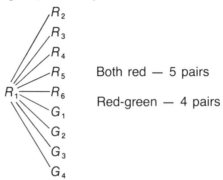

We can start the above tree with any of six different red marbles, so there will be $6 \times 4 = 24$ red-green pairs.

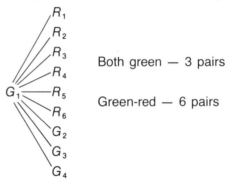

We can start this tree with any of four different green marbles, so there will be $4 \times 6 = 24$ green-red pairs.

Thus the probability of a pair with one red and one green is 48/90 or 8/15.

Another good discussion and an excellent calculator exercise is to play with the numbers of red and green marbles.

What happens to the probability as we increase the number of red marbles by one, and leave the number of green marbles the same? What is the decimal value of the probability in each case? Are the differences between successive probability values constant? Will the difference continue to decrease? When will the probability become zero?

Number red	Number green	Probability	Decimal value	Difference
6	4	8/15	0.5333	
7	4	28/55	0.5091	0.0242
8	4	16/33	0.4848	0.0243
9	4	6/13	0.4615	0.0233

Triangular numbers are numbers which can be represented by dots in an equilateral triangular array. The first four triangular numbers are shown below.

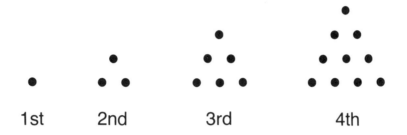

1st   2nd   3rd   4th

In the table below, n represents the number of dots on one side of the array, and T represents the total number of dots in the array. Complete the table through the 15th triangular number. What patterns do you see?

n	T
1	1
2	3
3	6
4	10
5	
6	
7	
8	
9	
10	
11	
12	
13	
14	
15	

Copyright © 1982 by Dale Seymour Publications.

15. WARM-UP

Answer:

n	T
1	1
2	3
3	6
4	10
5	15
6	21
7	28
8	36
9	45
10	55
11	66
12	78
13	91
14	105
15	120

Teaching Suggestions:

Encourage the students to find and discuss as many different patterns as they can. Every time I give this problem, it seems that at least one student describes a pattern that I've never heard described before. Some patterns are useful in extending the table one row at a time, but may not lead to a general formula for the nth triangular number. Occasionally, a student will find the pattern that the nth triangular number is half the product of n and $n + 1$ directly from the table.

Be sure that all the students understand how Gauss' technique can be used to find the sum of counting numbers. It's far less important that they remember the formula for triangular numbers than that they understand the means by which they can recreate the formula for themselves.

Solution:

There are many different patterns that students will discover in this table. Here are a few that my students have presented:

The 5th triangular number will be a triangle with 5 dots on each side; the nth triangular number array has n dots on each side.

The differences between successive triangular numbers keep increasing by one.

The 7th triangular number equals the 6th plus 7; the nth triangular number equals the $(n + 1)$th triangular number plus n.

The 6th triangular number is the sum $1 + 2 + 3 + 4 + 5 + 6$; the nth triangular number is the sum of the first n counting numbers.

This last observation can lead to a formula for finding the value of any triangular number. We need to make use once again of Gauss' summing technique.

$$1 + 2 + 3 + \ldots + (n - 2) + (n - 1) + n$$

There are $n/2$ pairs of numbers here, and each pair has a sum of $n + 1$. So the sum of all the pairs is

$$\frac{n}{2}(n + 1) \text{ or } \frac{n(n + 1)}{2},$$

which is the value of the nth triangular number.

In the Century City grocery store, all the oranges are stacked in triangular pyramids. Each layer of oranges is in the shape of an equilateral triangle, and the top layer is a single orange. How many oranges are in a stack ten layers high?

Copyright © 1982 by Dale Seymour Publications.

15. SUNSHINE PYRAMID

Answer: 220 oranges

Hint:

How many oranges are in each layer?

Solution:

First, we look at the individual layers in the triangular pyramid. A model or a drawing is helpful in counting the number of oranges in each layer.

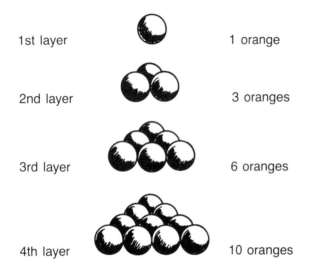

1st layer	1 orange
2nd layer	3 oranges
3rd layer	6 oranges
4th layer	10 oranges

This pattern should look familiar. It's the triangular number pattern we explored in the *Warm-up* problem. We can certainly list the first ten triangular numbers, and then find their sum.

$$1 + 3 + 6 + 10 + 15 + 21 + 28 + 36 + 45 + 55 = 220$$

So there are 220 oranges in a ten-layer triangular pyramidal stack.

Teaching Suggestions:

Here is another opportunity for students to "look back" and relate a problem to a previously-studied pattern.

An obvious extension is to look for a formula for the number of oranges in a stack *n* layers high. See the discussion of problem *16. Galactic Connection* for the development of this formula.

15. EXTENSION

Extend each of the following number sequences to the 10th term. Then find the 100th term, and write a formula that expresses the nth term of the sequence.

A. 2, 4, 6, 8, 10, _____, _____, _____, _____, _____,
   100th term _____ nth term _____

B. 1, 3, 5, 7, 9, _____, _____, _____, _____, _____,
   100th term _____ nth term _____

C. 3, 6, 9, 12, 15, _____, _____, _____, _____, _____,
   100th term _____ nth term _____

D. 7, 10, 13, 16, 19, _____, _____, _____, _____, _____,
   100th term _____ nth term _____

E. $\frac{3}{2}$, 2, $\frac{5}{2}$, 3, $\frac{7}{2}$, _____, _____, _____, _____, _____,
   100th term _____ nth term _____

F. 9, 23, 37, 51, 65, _____, _____, _____, _____, _____,
   100th term _____ nth term _____

Copyright © 1982 by Dale Seymour Publications.

Answer: A. 12, 14, 16, 18, 20; 200; $2n$
B. 11, 13, 15, 17, 19; 199; $2n - 1$
C. 18, 21, 24, 27, 30; 300; $3n$
D. 22, 25, 28, 31, 34; 304; $3n + 4$
E. 4, $\frac{9}{2}$, 5, $\frac{11}{2}$, 6; 51; $\dfrac{n + 2}{2}$
F. 79, 93, 107, 121, 135; 1395; $14n - 5$

Hint:

Can you find a relationship between the number of the term and its value?

Solution:

Some students may find it helpful to put the sequences into tables, and then compare the number n to the value of the nth term.

A. The sequence of even numbers is a very familiar one to students. But the younger students may never have thought about the pattern in this way before. Each term is two times the number of that term. The value of the nth term is $2 \times n$ or $2n$.

B. The sequence of odd numbers can be related to the sequence of even numbers. The nth odd number is one less than the nth even number. So a formula for the nth odd number is $2n - 1$.

C. The numbers in this sequence are all multiples of three, and the formula for the nth term is $3n$.

D. A table is helpful in finding the pattern for this sequence.

n	nth term
1	7
2	10
3	13
4	16
5	19

(constant difference of 3)

Extending the sequence through the tenth term is easy once the constant difference of 3 is noticed. But to find the 100th and nth terms is trickier. One way is to notice that each term but the first equals 7 plus a multiple of 3, or that each term including the first equals 4 plus a multiple of 3.

  1st: $4 + 1 \times 3$, 2nd: $4 + 2 \times 3$, 3rd: $4 + 3 \times 3$, and so on.
Thus, the nth term equals $4 + n \times 3$, or $3n + 4$.

E. Writing every term as an improper fraction shows a pattern of counting numbers in the numerators: $\frac{3}{2}$, $\frac{4}{2}$, $\frac{5}{2}$, $\frac{6}{2}$, ... Each numerator is two more than the number of that term. So the nth term in this sequence is $\dfrac{n + 2}{2}$.

F. The key to generalizing the pattern in this sequence is noticing that there is a constant difference of 14 between successive terms. Each term is the sum of some number and some multiple of 14. If we want the nth term to correspond to the nth multiple of 14, then the first term $9 = 1 \times 14 - 5$. The second term $23 = 2 \times 14 - 5$, and so on. So the value of the nth term is $14n - 5$.

Teaching Suggestions:

Looking for constant differences between successive terms in a sequence is part of the general technique of finite differences. For more activities using this technique, see *Finite Differences* by Seymour and Shedd, published in 1973 by Creative Publications, Palo Alto, California.

Some whole numbers can be written as a difference of two squares.
For example, $0 = 0^2 - 0^2$ and $8 = 3^2 - 1^2$. Try to write each of the first
26 whole numbers as a difference of two squares. Which numbers
cannot be written in this way?

Number	Difference of two squares
0	$0^2 - 0^2$
1	
2	
3	
4	
5	
6	
7	
8	$3^2 - 1^2$
9	
10	
11	
12	
13	
14	
15	
16	
17	
18	
19	
20	
21	
22	
23	
24	
25	

Copyright © 1982 by Dale Seymour Publications.

16. WARM-UP

Answer:

Number	Difference of two squares
0	$0^2 - 0^2$
1	$1^2 - 0^2$
2	?
3	$2^2 - 1^2$
4	$4^2 - 0^2$
5	$3^2 - 2^2$
6	?
7	$4^2 - 3^2$
8	$3^2 - 1^2$
9	$3^2 - 0^2$ or $5^2 - 4^2$
10	?
11	$6^2 - 5^2$
12	$4^2 - 2^2$
13	$7^2 - 6^2$
14	?
15	$4^2 - 1^2$ or $8^2 - 7^2$
16	$4^2 - 0^2$ or $5^2 - 3^2$
17	$9^2 - 8^2$
18	?
19	$10^2 - 9^2$
20	$6^2 - 4^2$
21	$5^2 - 2^2$ or $11^2 - 10^2$
22	?
23	$12^2 - 11^2$
24	$5^2 - 1^2$
25	$5^2 - 0^2$

The numbers that cannot be represented as the difference of two squares are 2, 6, 10, 14, 18, 22, ... These are numbers of the form $4n + 2$.

Hint:

Make a list of perfect squares.

Solution:

A list of perfect squares from 1 to 196 is helpful in solving this problem. The solutions are found by trial and error.

Teaching Suggestions:

Two interesting patterns should be discussed.

Notice the set of odd numbers. These can be represented as a difference of squares as shown below.

n	Odd number $2n - 1$	Difference of squares
1	1	$1^2 - 0^2$
2	3	$2^2 - 1^2$
3	5	$3^2 - 2^2$
4	7	$4^2 - 3^2$
.		
.		
.		
n	$2n - 1$	$n^2 - (n - 1)^2$

Notice the set of all even numbers of the form $4n$.

n	$4n$	Difference of squares
0	0	$1^2 - (-1)^2$
1	4	$2^2 - 0^2$
2	8	$3^2 - 1^2$
3	12	$4^2 - 2^2$
.		
.		
.		
n	$4n$	$(n + 1)^2 - (n - 1)^2$

92

There are nine points in a plane. No three points are in the same straight line. How many different triangles can be formed by using the nine points as vertices?

Copyright © 1982 by Dale Seymour Publications.

16. GALACTIC CONNECTION

Answer: 84 triangles

Hint:

How many triangles can be formed using three points as vertices? Four points? Five points?

Solution:

Students who try to draw and count all the different triangles formed using nine points as vertices will soon realize the difficulty of this approach. A better approach, and one that is often helpful in solving problems, is to look at related simpler problems. Beginning with just three points as vertices, list the triangles formed and try to see some patterns that will shorten the counting process.

3 points	Triangles
A • C • • B	ABC 1 triangle

4 points	Triangles
A • • B C • • D	ABC, ABD, ACD BCD 3 + 1 = 4 triangles

5 points	Triangles
A • E • • B D • • C	ABC, ABD, ABE, ACD, ACE, ADE BCD, BCE, BDE CDE 6 + 3 + 1 = 10 triangles

6 points	Triangles
A • F • • B E • • C • D	ABC, ABD, ABE, ABF, ACD, ACE, ACF, ADE, ADF, AEF BCD, BCE, BCF, BDE, BDF, BEF CDE, CDF, CEF DEF 10 + 6 + 3 + 1 = 20 triangles

Students may continue to count and list the number of triangles as we have done in the first four examples. Most, however, will try to determine a pattern. By examining the differences, the pattern can be continued as shown in the table below.

Number of points	Number of triangles
3	1
4	4
5	10
6	20
7	35
8	56
9	(84)

Those students who have worked with triangular numbers before will recognize the first set of differences as the triangular number sequence 1, 3, 6, 10, 15, ...

Teaching Suggestions:

In order for students to have success in this problem, it is most important that they examine the simplest problem first, and then develop the table. They will notice many patterns as the solution develops.

One pattern they should observe is that in listing the number of triangles formed by six points, the number formed with AB is 4, with AC is 3, with AD is 2, and with AE is 1. This pattern continues in the remaining cases.

A few students will be able to discover a formula for the sequence 1, 4, 10, 20, 35, 56, 84, ... Others can obtain the formula with a little help from the technique of finite differences. The formula to be discovered is

$$\frac{n^3 + 3n^2 + 2n}{6} \quad \text{or} \quad \frac{n(n+1)(n+2)}{6}.$$

We want to start our table with the number of points being three, and generate the sequence 1, 4, 10, 35, ... To do that creates a nice algebraic manipulation. We must subtract two from the number of points in each case. Thus, $n(n+1)(n+2)$ becomes

$$(n-2)((n-2)+1)((n-2)+2)$$
$$= (n-2)(n-1)(n)$$
$$= (n^2 - 3n + 2)n$$
$$= n^3 - 3n^2 + 2n$$

So the formula for the number of triangles generated in each case is $\dfrac{n^3 - 3n^2 + 2n}{6}$.

Given square ABCD with sides of length 2. Diagonals AC and BD intersect at M. Points E, F, G, and H are the midpoints of AM, BM, CM, and DM respectively. Points J and K are the midpoints of CD and AB respectively. Find the area of the hexagon JHEKFG.

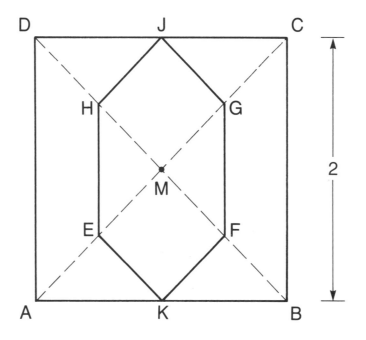

Copyright © 1982 by Dale Seymour Publications.

16. EXTENSION

Answer: 3/2 or 1 1/2

Hint:

Look for congruent triangles.

Solution:

From the Pythagorean theorem, we know that if the sides of the triangle ABD are 2, then $BD = \sqrt{2^2 + 2^2} = 2\sqrt{2}$. Therefore, $DM = \sqrt{2}$ and $HM = \frac{\sqrt{2}}{2}$. Because the diagonals of the square form right angles, we can use the Pythagorean theorem again to find the lengths HE, HG, GF, and FE to be

$$\sqrt{\left(\frac{\sqrt{2}}{2}\right)^2 + \left(\frac{\sqrt{2}}{2}\right)^2} = \sqrt{\frac{2}{4} + \frac{2}{4}} = 1.$$

Thus, the square EFGH has an area of $1 \times 1 = 1$.

My students created many variations of the following lines of reasoning. The four isosceles right triangles HMG, GMF, FME, and EMH are all congruent, and are also congruent to triangles HJG and FKE. So the area of triangle HJG and of triangle FKE is one-quarter the area of the square HGFE. Thus, the area of the hexagon JHEKFG is
$1 + \frac{1}{4} + \frac{1}{4} = \frac{3}{2}$ or $1\frac{1}{2}$.

Teaching Suggestions:

It is essential to consider this problem in parts. Review carefully the properties of the diagonals of a square, the angles formed, and the fact that the diagonals bisect each other.

Other solution method that my students have used is to rotate the hexagon 90° forming a second hexagon and dividing the square into 16 congruent right triangles.

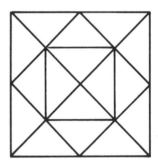

The original hexagon JHEKFG contains 6 of those triangles and therefore represents 6/16 or 3/8 of the total area of the square. The area of square ABCD is 2 × 2 = 4. So the area of the hexagon is 4 × 3/8 = 12/8 = 3/2. (The congruence of the triangles can be demonstrated nicely by folding a model of the square.)

This problem is suitable for use with a geoboard. Use different colored rubber bands and start with simply a square. Your students will develop intuitively a host of theorems and definitions of geometry.